> INTO THE FIRE

> INTO THE FIRE

A POST-9/11 AMERICAN IN TEL AVIV

Charles T. Salmon

Michigan State University Press • *East Lansing*

Michigan State University Press
East Lansing, Michigan 48823-5245

Printed and bound in the United States of America.

09 08 07 06 05 04 03   1 2 3 4 5 6 7 8 9 10

LIBRARY OF CONGRESS CATALOGING-IN-PUBLICATION DATA
Salmon, Charles T. (Charles Thomas)
Into the fire : a post-9/11 American in Tel Aviv / Charles T. Salmon.
p. cm.
Includes bibliographical references.
ISBN 0-87013-695-X (pbk. : alk. paper)
1. Salmon, Charles T. (Charles Thomas)—Journeys—Israel—Tel Aviv.
2. Tel Aviv (Israel)—Description and travel. 3. Arab-Israeli conflict—1993–
I. Title: Post-9/11 American in Tel Aviv. II. Title.
DS110.T34S34 2003
956.9405'4'092—dc21
2003009750

Cover design by Erin Kirk New
Book design by Sharp Des!gns, Inc., Lansing, MI

Visit Michigan State University Press on the World Wide Web at: *www.msupress.msu.edu*

CONTENTS

ACKNOWLEDGMENTS

AN ODYSSEY SUCH AS MINE could never have been completed without the help of numerous guides along the way, all of whom generously offered their time, patience, support, wisdom, insights, and/or friendship many times over (but none of whom, of course, is responsible for any errors of fact or interpretation that I, a complete outsider to Israeli culture, may have made in this work). I am grateful to all, and yet, at the risk of offending, have space to single out but a few, starting with my extraordinary palindromic host family of Guttmans/ Krameks—Nurit, Bob, Oren, Benny, and Niva—who spent countless hours and went to unprecedented lengths to ensure that my stay was a productive and enjoyable one. I also owe a debt of gratitude to my students in "Mass Communication and Public Opinion," as well as to Dafna Lemish, Akiba Cohen, and the entire faculty and staff of the Department of Communication at Tel Aviv University; and to Vered Seidmann, Jacob and Michal Shamir, Linda-Renee Bloch, Carmel Shalev, Hannah Peleg, Boaz Lev, Yair Amikam, and Sylvie Honigman.

Closer to home, I would like to thank Jim Spaniolo for his considerable support throughout this project, and Lou Anna Simon, Ned Brandt and the Gerstacker Foundation, Mark Levy, Steve Weiland, Ted Glasser, Kathleen and Brian Kelleher, and Galen Cole. Special thanks as well go to Martha Bates, Menahem Blondheim, and Avner Segall for their helpful comments on an earlier draft of this manuscript.

Finally, I would like to thank the U.S. and Israeli offices of the Fulbright Foundation (and Judy Stavsky and Gary Garrison in particular) for making this opportunity possible in the first place. As far as I am concerned, the Fulbright program has no equal, and we are all a little better off as result of its many unseen daily contributions to international understanding and cooperation.

PROLOGUE

FOR MOST OF MY professional life, I had dreamed of winning a Fulbright Fellowship and traveling to some exotic land in which to teach, learn, and conduct research. Although an Irish Catholic with only a passing familiarity with Jewish culture, I was fascinated with Israel's history and politics, and hoped that an opportunity there would become available just as I would be stepping down from four long years of work in academic administration. As fate would have it, such an opportunity did arise, and in my first attempt, I worked through the highly competitive process and was awarded a Fulbright in the Department of Communication at Tel Aviv University, beginning in September, 2001. But first, there were a few loose ends to tie up.

Several weeks before I was to leave for Israel, I was enjoying the late summer weather of Oslo and lecturing about persuasive communication and my new research area: bioterrorism preparedness. At one colloquium, most of my audience of faculty and graduate students listened with polite interest, but a few were openly skeptical. Wasn't the alleged threat of bioterrorism merely another transparent attempt by the U.S. government to manufacture a new enemy in the geopolitical vacuum created by the demise of the Soviet Union? Wasn't this science fiction masquerading as justification for the Defense Department to secure more funding? While acknowledging that the threat was of low probability, I did cite the warnings of several prominent politicians, from all parts of the political spectrum, who sincerely believed that a terrorist attack involving biological weapons was imminent.

On September 9, 2001, I faxed the finishing touches on a telephone survey of bioterrorism preparedness that was to start the next day in the States, boarded my flight, and arrived in Michigan just in time to unpack, do laundry, and repack before my next flight was to leave for Tel Aviv on the thirteenth.

Or so I thought.

It's difficult even now, more than one year later, to accurately convey how we as a nation, and I as a frequent global traveler felt when those three airplanes struck the World Trade Center and the Pentagon. Terror, disbelief, shock, horror, fear— no word satisfactorily captures what I was feeling on that day, especially knowing that my flight for Tel Aviv was scheduled to depart only two days later. I was in a panic, and the situation was completely chaotic. I was scheduled to depart from Chicago, a drive of some three or four hours away, but could not get through to the airline staff to find out what was happening. The phone lines were constantly jammed; the airline website had little to offer. After repeated calls, the travel agent who originally had booked the flight took my name and number, and said that new arrangements would be made—that is, if I still wanted to fly. "Of course!" I blurted out, without fully appreciating the consequences of my words, and rebooked my flight for

September 29. I figured that this later date would give law enforcement groups enough time to get their act together and restore safety to the skies. But the more I thought about it, the less comfortable I was with the idea of flying—let alone flying out of the frying pan that was post–9/11 America and into the fire of the Middle East.

In the days that followed, I experienced a crisis of faith—the magnitude of which I had not encountered in years. I became absolutely, totally convinced that I would die on this trip, either in a fiery explosion in the air, or from an errant bullet or fragment of bomb shrapnel on the ground. With every passing day, I came closer and closer to declining my fellowship and remaining in the United States. I contacted the Fulbright office and found the staff to be supportive and sympathetic. While they couldn't guarantee that I would be able to get a Fulbright in the future, they said they would understand if I was too uncomfortable to continue with this one. But the bottom line was that they encouraged me to go through with the trip and assured me that all Fulbrighters would be evacuated in the event of a genuine crisis, if that was indeed any consolation. In addition, they put me in touch with a couple of American academics already in Israel, one of whom responded by saying that things were generally fine. How could that be, I wondered, in the midst of a bloody intifada? When all I saw on television and read in the papers was about bombs, bullets, and angry politicians? What else was there to do over there, I wondered, other than duck behind walls, get out of the way of tanks, or anxiously await news of the latest act of terrorism?

Not satisfied with this advice, I sought additional perspective and counsel. A quick check of the U.S. State Department website showed that Americans were being advised to defer travel to Israel because of the threat of danger to U.S. citizens in the region. Why, then—I thought to myself—were American Fulbrighters being encouraged to violate State Department directives? My own university, which prides itself on having one of the most elaborate "Study Abroad" programs in the country, was suspending its program in Israel because of the presumed danger to students. Not a good sign, either. Women friends unanimously advised me (sometimes using stronger terms) to stay, and most told me I was crazy for even considering going in the current global climate. Most male friends, in contrast, were far more likely to say that they would still go if they could; but of course, they couldn't, and so I discounted some of their claims as little more than bravado. An Israeli friend simply lost patience with me. "Americans are such wimps!" she said on the phone, continuing on about how silly it was for us to be so paralyzed by one act of terrorism when Israelis lived normal lives in the midst of a constant threat of terrorism. I bristled with resentment upon hearing these words. Clearly, I thought to myself in pure, unadulterated egocentrism, after September 11, nobody but an American was capable of understanding what it felt like to be the victim of terrorism.

Jewish-American academic friends said that they empathized with my concerns, but encouraged me to give it a try. One patiently sat with me and helped me work through the implications of what would happen if terrorists were to use shoulder-mounted missiles to shoot down commercial jetliners in Tel Aviv. True, I wouldn't be able to leave the country by air, and fleeing by car to unfriendly Arab borders would pose its own special risks. But I could always grab a boat and paddle into the Mediterranean Sea! Impressive ingenuity, to be sure, but a disconcertingly mixed message—matched by an equally disconcerting parting gift: a copy of *The Complete Idiot's Guide to Jewish History and Culture.*

All of this advice and perspective was useful, but—like Woody Allen's character experiencing his own crisis of faith in the movie *Annie Hall*—I yearned for some deeper reassurance. For the first time in my life, I made out my will, writing it by hand according to instructions in a "do-it-yourself" kit of legal documents. Next, I made a list of all the people with whom I had outstanding problems or unresolved issues, and decided that I needed to gain some resolution in this part of my life. I didn't consider myself an especially religious person; indeed, a friend of mine once joked that I was merely one of many "recovering Catholics" stumbling through life. But something about this trip was triggering feelings deep inside a core that I didn't even know existed within me. I visited an energetic and optimistic young priest and talked about my crisis of faith, and especially how I was so upset with myself for being afraid of dying. How could I call myself a Christian if I didn't have any faith and was full of fear? I asked. What made me feel worse were media reports describing how the devout Muslim terrorists had been willing to face death by ramming an airplane into a building at high speed for the sake of their own faith and ideals. And here I was, afraid to face life and board a plane at all. I was frankly disgusted with myself, as well as concerned for my fellow citizens because our faith was not as strong as that of the Muslim terrorists. As I wrote in confidence to a friend:

> To me, the decision has become an issue of faith; a choice between materialism and spirituality; an inner struggle that, ironically, mirrors the Taliban's depiction of the current global crisis. If I profess to be a Christian and to believe in eternal realities greater than those of the ephemeral material world, but I do not have faith, then what do I really have? Words are cheap, but actions require faith. In many ways, I

am disappointed in myself for even hesitating to go forward, for it reveals a spiritual flaw in my human composition. And so, I wrestle with these matters while the metaphysical wars rage within. . . .

This was an especially difficult e-mail for me, a social scientist in a community of scholars who often view religion and spirituality with great suspicion and cynicism, to send to a fellow academic. Cracks were beginning to show in the walls surrounding my well-disguised spiritual upbringing.

I don't remember any one specific turning point, but momentum eventually just took over. My new departure date was September 29, and about a week before that date I found myself sorting my books and clothes, packing out of instinct and habit, rather than conscious decision. Friends would come up to me and say, "You're not still going, are you?" and I would bravely reply, "Yeah, I'm going to give it a try." And so it became a self-fulfilling prophecy; I couldn't back out now. As my departure date neared, I actually began feeling more and more at peace with my decision. Visions of burning in a plane were replaced with images of exotic sights and sounds. Concern about personal safety gave way to anticipation and curiosity about meeting new friends, engaging in exciting adventures, and developing a more sophisticated understanding of this volatile and highly important corner of the world. My mood lightened considerably, and I felt as though I could accept any outcome that might happen. Just in case, though, I did get a prescription for anti-anxiety medication, for use in the event of a panic attack on the airplane during the grueling overseas flights to Paris and then to Tel Aviv.

On the morning of September 29, I drove to my sister and

nephew's apartment in Kalamazoo. We had a pleasant reunion, and I gave them a copy of my will, the key to my safe deposit box, and instructions for my funeral service that even included specific music to be played at the reception, and detailed instructions for dispersal of my ashes following cremation. With my corporal accounts now as settled as my spiritual ones, I was ready to go. My nephew drove me to O'Hare Airport in Chicago, an unusually quiet and somber place compared to previous visits. Although I was expecting horrible delays and thorough examinations of my bags, I was shocked to be whisked through security with little more than a glance. I didn't have to prove that my laptop computer wasn't actually a bomb, nor did I even have to reveal the contents of my bag to anyone. I remember actually feeling disappointed at the ease and rapidity with which I was ushered to the waiting area. Nevertheless, after years of dreaming of this opportunity, tempered by weeks of excruciating anguish in the wake of 9/11, my Middle Eastern Fulbright adventure was about to begin.

· · ·

What follows are letters from Israel, sent weekly via e-mail, describing life in Tel Aviv during the Second Intifada (or Palestinian uprising), which was already nearly a year old when I arrived. More than anything else, my letters were motivated by three distinct factors: (1) my feelings of sheer ecstasy at trading East Lansing, Michigan, for the stimulating, exotic, and sunny environment of Tel Aviv; (2) my astonishment at seeing the vast discrepancy between life in Israel experienced first-hand versus life in Israel as portrayed in American newspapers and TV news shows; (3) my desire to learn how a group of people could maintain some semblance of normal life while in the throes of daily terrorist activities. Having just experienced the tragedy of September 11, this last point seemed all the more important at the time.

> INTO THE FIRE

WEEK 1: GENESIS

SO LIFE IS OKAY here on the balmy Mediter-
ranean, in spite of what CNN may say. The trip was thankfully
uneventful, though one of the two main airports in Paris (Orly)
closed due to a bomb scare when our plane entered French air-
space. Fortunately, we were headed to the other, DeGaulle, and
landed in thick, *Casablanca*-like fog at 6 A.M. In Paris, airport
security was about as formidable as Michigan State University's
football defense on Saturday;* when an inquisitive child tried to
crawl through the x-ray machine, the lone security guard ran
around to pull her out, leaving bags and people streaming
through unattended. Fortunately, no terrorists appeared to be
lurking nearby.

After a trip of some twenty-six hours, I fell asleep to soft
Mediterranean breezes, only to awaken when some Pantera-
wannabe started playing an electric guitar at 2 or 3 A.M. I awoke

---

*In a development that shocked (Michigan State) Spartan fans in East Lansing and beyond,
Northwestern University moved eighty-seven yards in fourteen seconds to win, 27–26, a game
marked by three lead changes in the final twenty-eight seconds.

a second time to the sounds of horse hooves and a loudspeaker in the streets. Having just arrived from the paranoia that is the United States, realizing that the one-year anniversary of the intifada had just occurred, and speaking no Hebrew, I naturally assumed that we were under chemical attack and were being advised to flee to the basement immediately. I later learned that it was merely an Arab roaming the streets in search of used furniture to purchase.

My Macintosh laptop, as was the case in Norway, is a thing of mystery to my computer-literate friends, and so I will be frequenting the many local cyber cafés in the days and evenings to come. One such café, up near Dizengoff Center, is a clean and well-lighted place, with modern flat-screen monitors, a bar, and lots of young people wearing headphones and playing video games.

Life is actually quite normal and peaceful in Tel Aviv. Dogs sans leashes roam the streets, hundreds (thousands?) of cats peruse well-stocked dumpsters, and people instinctively dodge the many dog-droppings that litter the sidewalks; pooper-scoopers do not yet seem to have diffused this far. On most blocks, huge yellow iron bins can be found in which people voluntarily recycle their plastic bottles. As a security measure, the bins have bars for sides, so that their contents can be easily viewed from outside, and small openings into which bottles must fit, a design that limits their use for hidden bombs. Speaking of bombs, security guards routinely screen customers heading into malls. Yesterday I went to a local mall near Rabin Square and was approached by a somber security guard. He looked at me, looked in my shopping bag, looked at me again, said something to me in Hebrew, and finally said in halting English, "You . . . Have . . . Gun?" I assured him that I did not, and he seemed both relieved and satisfied with my response.

I'm staying in downtown Tel Aviv, about fifteen minutes from the Opera Hall, ten minutes from the Mediterranean Sea, and closer still to "New York Restaurant," home of the self-acclaimed "best steak in Tel Aviv." My flat, in an eleven-unit building, is on a narrow, tree-lined street, rendered narrower still by two rows of parked cars, many of which are squeezed at ridiculous angles into meager spaces, resting as much on the sidewalk as on the street. The neighborhood is typical for this part of Tel Aviv: three- and four-story, light-colored stucco buildings, showing their age through cracks, rough plaster patches, and sand-colored stains. Most of the buildings are supported by three or four square pillars, creating spaces in which animals—and now cars—have been known to be parked over the years. White and black iron grills, sun porches, and flower boxes adorn the upper floors of many of the buildings, as do occasional clotheslines weighted down with soggy laundry. From the rooftops jut antiquated broadcast antennae, tendrils of black wires, and multiple white canisters—water heaters for the various flats contained within.

My one-bedroom apartment is charming, though eerily reminiscent of bland faculty housing. It is decorated in early minimalist style, with a bed, desk, and chair, and a homemade sofa formed by a narrow mattress resting on plastic supports. The building lobby looks like something out of an old Chicago gangster film: dark, dirty, dimly lit by bulbs on a brief timer, with a winding staircase that creates far too many nooks and crannies in which a mobster could hide with his Tommy gun. But this is Tel Aviv, not Chicago, and so people don't get afraid when the hallways are plunged into total darkness, instead just grumbling as their hands grope along the walls in search of a switch to restore light. Like most flats here, my home has a wonderful sun porch with distinctive horizontal shutters characteristic of Tel Aviv, no screens on the windows, and a long wait for hot water.

Soon after my arrival, news of a car bomb explosion in Jerusalem reaches Tel Aviv and temporarily disrupts my Mediterranean fantasy. I know this only because at a certain point in the evening, I hear the sound of radios and television sets being turned on in unison throughout my apartment building. Since I speak and understand only one word of Hebrew ("shalom"), this sound is my signal that I need to turn on the television or call a friend to find out what newsworthy event has just occurred somewhere in the country.

Over the years, we have taught thousands of young journalism students the classic definition of news: when dog bites person, it's not news; when person bites dog, it's news. By this definition, news inherently distorts, emphasizing the atypical and unrepresentative while ignoring the ordinary and routine. We have also conditioned our students to look for "bad" news and to be skeptical of "good" news, especially if the latter emanates from self-serving government or corporate sources. Though I've studied these media processes and biases for years, their full impact didn't really hit home until this week. Yes, there are bombings here—in fact, tonight I visited the disco where a suicide bomber killed twenty young people a couple of months ago. Yet, in spite of the impression gleaned from network newscasts, life is as normal here as in any large city in the world. Surfers are flocking to the beaches, because the waves are huge with the recent full moon and resulting change in tides. Soccer fans are gearing up for this weekend's World Cup qualifying match with Austria. Families are enjoying the holiday week,* grilling chicken in their backyards. Couples stroll along the

*People are celebrating Succot, a holiday that commemorates the ancient Israelites' exodus from Egypt.

boardwalk and sandy beach on their way to Jaffa for dinner. The magnificent opera house is featuring a Russian version of *Hamlet*, while the nearby museum is promoting a "Jazz Bach" concert this weekend. Cafés are crowded, as is the three-pool natatorium during this holiday season. People are perhaps a little more vigilant about looking for unattended packages and strange-looking backpacks, but my guess is that Americans may soon be adopting this same degree of vigilance as well. Given the disparity of images between what we see in the United States and what happens here on a day-to-day basis, it's amazing that any of our perceptions of Israel—or any other country, for that matter—are remotely accurate. Life goes on, and for tonight at least, I am safe and sound. I wish the same for all of you back in the States in the weeks to come . . .

WEEK 2: REFLECTIONS

HOW THE WORLD HAS CHANGED since my
note of one week ago. Bombs now rain down in the Afghani
night sky; anti-American sentiments percolate throughout the
Middle East; a Palestinian disguised in the garb of an Israeli soldier slipped into a community and shot several unsuspecting
citizens; and a plane departing from Tel Aviv was struck by a
Ukranian missile over the Black Sea, killing all aboard. A very
sad week in many respects, but nevertheless, life goes on here
in Israel.

On Tuesday, a ceremony signifying "joy of Torah" marked
the end of a long holiday season. At the local synagogue, I
donned my bright red polyester skull cap (which instantly and
unmistakably identified me as a tourist), headed to an upstairs
room where women weren't allowed, and watched in wonder-
ment as dozens of boys and young men danced in a circle,
singing loudly, clapping, carrying large and ornately decorated
containers, and generally having a wonderful time. From what
I understand, during the previous year the young men had read

every line of the Torah, and now they would celebrate with abandon until having to start all over again from line 1 with the advent of the new year.

Outside, the streets were deserted all day, which is actually a good thing. As dangerous as terrorism is, driving is worse. Far more Israelis are killed in traffic accidents than in suicide bombings, though you'd never know that from CNN. Automobiles are quite expensive here, as are automobile repairs, and yet fender benders and other assorted accidents are rampant. Drivers seem to be in a great hurry all the time, looking for that slight edge that might allow them to arrive at their destination a millisecond or two early—or, more likely, to get into an accident.

I haven't quite figured out why people are in such a hurry. Back in the States, a Jewish friend told me that there were two Hebrew phrases I wouldn't have to bother to learn over here: "thank you" and "excuse me." Actually, it turns out that Hebrew for "excuse me" can also be interpreted as "get out of my way," which is indeed a valuable phrase to know. Impatience is manifested in many facets of everyday life. Developers of one local shopping mall were so impatient that they opened it before the building was finished, leaving customers to dodge the falling debris as they (quickly) entered and exited the stores. People regularly cut in line at the airport, supermarkets, and ticket windows. Even while standing in line for communion at the Catholic church in Jaffa, I could feel people behind me lightly pushing and jostling for position, apparently unable to restrain their eagerness to taste spiritual salvation.

Television programming is far more interesting here than in the States. With channels from a number of European and Middle Eastern countries, there is no shortage of diversity of perspective. Analysis of current events is richer, more sophisticated, and more plentiful than back in central Michigan. No surprise there. And yet, there is an amazing amount of similarity as well, as multiple versions of *Who Wants to Be a Millionaire?* flood the airwaves. Arabs wearing traditional *kaffya*, Russians in suits, and more casually dressed Israelis (to name only a few of the nationalities) all carefully allocate their lifelines as they attempt to answer questions from Regis Philbin clones—most of whom are younger and more serious. The single most pervasive image of the United States on TV? It would have to be Michael Jackson and his music video "You Rock My World," which is playing at any given moment, twenty-four hours a day, on some Middle Eastern or European channel. Coverage of ice hockey, unfortunately, isn't high on broadcasters' playlists, not even games that set world records in attendance;* soccer is the undisputed king of Middle Eastern sport.

My one major adventure of the week occurred when my hosts and good friends drove me to Abu Ghosh, an Arab village nestled in the hills outside of Jerusalem. Our mission? To find the reputed best hummus in Israel. Still very much in my September 11 frame of mind, my heart started racing as our car headed up the winding hill, past modest stone houses with light-colored roofs (in contrast with roofs of Jewish homes, which tend to be red tile instead) and dusty, sandy yards. We parked the car and walked the gauntlet past cafés full of bearded Arab men—any one of whom could have been Osama bin Laden himself—sitting at tables, talking among themselves, and eying the three of us. I suddenly felt out of place, very American, and totally vulnerable. My hosts were surprised and a bit amused by my discomfort; after all, they said, this was a friendly and totally safe Arab village, and there was absolutely no reason to be nervous. But to

---

*Earlier this week, Michigan State University and the University of Michigan combined to set an attendance record for a game of ice hockey, drawing some 64,554 fans to witness a 2–2 tie at Spartan Stadium.

me, this was a classic case of a distinction without a difference: an Arab village was an Arab village, and—short of being in Afghanistan—I couldn't imagine having put myself in a more precarious situation. But in the end, my hosts were right, as usual. We shopped in safety, and I even learned a valuable lesson in pronunciation: when in the Middle East and talking to Arab clerks, it's important to take great pains to emphasize that you are searching for "hummus," not "Hamas."

My second week here has coincided with the one-month anniversary of September 11, and tonight I was one of ten Israeli, Arab, and American poets/writers/artists invited to share our words and feelings at a memorial service dedicated to the tragedy. The service, sponsored by the newly arrived American cultural attaché, was held in a magnificent villa in Kfar Shmar-yahu, a wealthy suburb where well-heeled American executives and their families enjoy their temporary Mediterranean assignments. It was a memorable evening, as men and women of diverse cultures took turns standing at a podium in a beautiful outdoor garden, adorned with small white lights and rows of chairs, and shared words of sadness, empathy, insight, inspiration, and hope. Some read their own published work: poems written for other purposes that resonated keenly with the topic at hand. One or two spoke of losses in their own lives or among their own people. Several shared their recollections of how they felt upon first hearing the news, whether in Israel or as tourists in America. When my name was called, I struggled to my feet and moved slowly to the podium. This wasn't the typical detached academic lecture that I could give extemporaneously; this was an expression of emotion from the heart, one that had taken days to write as I discarded draft after draft. My voice quavered ever so slightly as I began my comments with a statement that I was glad to be in Israel, and an explanation of what I would be doing here in the months to come. Following this brief introduction, I read my remarks:

The Day Before, Then, and Now

I sometimes find myself thinking wistfully back to September 10, 2001: an unremarkable Monday, a day that is forever relegated to the shadow of its far more prominent successor.

Little did we realize at the time that September 10 was actually a delicious wine to be savored—slowly, thoroughly, appreciatively. Instead, most of us gulped it down, unprepared for the imminent loss of our naiveté, our innocence, and our belief in an inalienable right to comfort and security that is so quintessentially American.

Of course, we found things about which to complain. An airport traveler in Boston undoubtedly groused about having to wait an extra minute when her wristwatch triggered the metal detector alarm.

A photographer, standing on the observation deck of a prominent New York City skyscraper, likely cursed his luck when the weather refused to cooperate with his photo shoot.

And in a small flat in Brooklyn, a young boy may have resented his father, a New York City fireman, for making him do his homework in the first week of the new school year.

It was, in other words, a typical American day. But who among us wouldn't gladly exchange our concerns of the present for those of that day?

Now, that same traveler at Logan Airport—if she is even willing to brave flying at all—walks nervously toward the metal detector, hoping that airport security will make her wait longer in line if it means a more thorough search of the suspicious stranger walking in front of her.

The frustrated photographer just sits and stares in disbelief at the ruin and destruction that now lies in a tangled mess where majestic towers once stood.

And somewhere in Brooklyn, a little boy who resented his father now sobs at the thought of him lying crushed under tons of fiery steel and concrete, and wishes only that he could see him one last time.

Rarely in our lifetime will we ever again pause to remember September 10 and the specifics of what we were doing, feeling, or complaining about that day. But every day, in its own way, is September 10: a day to be savored slowly, thoroughly, and appreciatively—the eve of one era and the dawn of another—and a day to be grateful for what we have, to enjoy the sight of a beautiful building, and to spend time with someone we love.

As I sign off from my cyber café terminal on this quiet Friday evening in downtown Tel Aviv, I send my wishes for a safe weekend. We have heard a lot about terse FBI warnings in the last day or two, and with today being the anniversary of the attack on the USS *Cole*, people here are concerned for the safety of their American friends. How the world has changed, indeed. As recently as two months ago, you probably couldn't have imagined hearing something like that from someone over here.

WEEK 3: THE BEACH

FOR THE FIRST TIME since my arrival, I had an official Fulbright experience, attending an orientation session sponsored by the Israeli Fulbright Foundation. At the session, the head of security for the American Embassy warned us of the potential dangers that await in our new land. Embassy employees aren't allowed to take buses, and are advised against being around crowds. In Tel Aviv, I guess that means we're supposed to eat bad food at unpopular restaurants and never go out on the streets. The native Israelis have a more moderate and realistic view, perhaps reflecting more experience with terrorism than we have in the States. I may be picking up on a Mediterranean rather than specifically Israeli way of life, but it does seem that there is greater acceptance of unpredictability and risk here than in the States, where we insist on trying to control so many aspects of our health and life—and regularly believe that we have the power to do so.

Heading south on Tel Aviv Beach, now home to a magnificent spectacle of sights, sounds, and smells. It's late afternoon—sunny, muggy, with a temperature in the high 70s—and about sixty middle-aged Israeli men and women are dancing in unison to loudly played traditional folk music, using dance steps that many learned as young students. A crowd of spectators gathers to watch, clap, and occasionally join in one of the dances, which bear some small resemblance to American line dancing, but at a faster pace with more subtle movements, better music, and no cowboy boots. An enormous red sun is oozing into the horizon, while forty or so one-person sailboats are bobbing and zipping along on the sea. White plastic chairs dot the beach, with a few stuck out on sandbars, beckoning adventurous bathers to cross the water to reach them. Closer in, several pairs of men play *matkot*, which is probably best described as beach paddle tennis without lines, nets, or designer athletic shoes.

It's early by Tel Aviv standards, and so the cafés are empty along the sandy sidewalk that parallels the beach. Farther down, with darkness settling in, the boom of drums starts filling the air. About twenty teenagers are beating African, Asian, and South American drums on a small, rocky knoll overlooking the beach, while down below, about a hundred teens are dancing, milling about, or just talking. A few highly proficient youngsters are jumping, crawling, and rolling on the sand while twirling cords, which have fiery ends, to the rhythmic and hypnotic beat of the drums. The fiery cords whip and whirl like tracers on a leash, flashing streaks of patterned light throughout the night sky.

In Jaffa now—where a fish restaurant lures prospective patrons with a sign that says "See Food." Cats that crowd around the outdoor tables appear like long-lost friends and peer at me longingly, hoping for a morsel of the fresh fish that they know is on the table. Well-dressed couples are arriving in taxis and expensive European cars, heading inside to set up for some apparently gala affair. Suddenly, as a man and woman walk up the steps, the inside of the café becomes pitch black, only to light up again, accompanied by the sudden din of shouting. Two European tourists immediately come running out, confused at the unexpected blackout and subsequent racket. Informed by the waiters that it is only a Russian wedding reception, the two men head back in to finish their drinks. After dinner, I walk past the many fishing vessels in the harbor and then see a larger boat moored to the dock, with music blaring from inside—a floating party on a rented boat for dozens of children, who are dancing and running around.

Walking around the old part of Jaffa now—a mixed city of Arabs and Jews where dozens of (wealthy) artists of all kinds now inhabit the ancient walls where Napoleon once stood in 1799. A winding maze of stairs and corridors leads to the sound of new and unfamiliar music. I head toward it, and it turns out to be a public café reserved for an Islamic pre-wedding party. Though nervous at the idea of crashing a private Muslim reception, especially as it's Friday, and Muslims have been attending religious services and getting more and more fired up about America's role in the Afghani crisis, the enticement of the unfamiliar music is too great, and so I ask (or really gesture with my hands) if I can stay and listen. I'm allowed to go to a porch overlooking the music. Down below, about fifty Muslim women are dancing to the strains of lively traditional Arab music, while the men on the porch look on. Most of the women are in traditional Muslim dress, though three or four are decked out in fabulous, sparkling, (Western) designer gowns, outfits that would rival anything worn in Cannes or Monaco. A couple of Muslim men stand close behind me, and I'm getting a little uncomfortable—until one of them sets before me a huge plate of baklava, a bowl of fruit, and a can of Sprite. Apparently, this is a gesture of hospitality, and despite several attempts to decline, I am now their guest and should not refuse. Conditioned by my heightened awareness of bioterrorism, I gingerly sample a few of the baked wares, but chug the Sprite before politely slipping out to allow the families the opportunity to celebrate without intruders.

Heading back north on the beach now, I pass a candlelit memorial to the twenty young people killed in the disco bombing. A grieving father stands and sobs, placing a small flower at the base of a stone memorial. Photos of the victims surround the stone, with a new photo added only today: that of Rehavem Zeevi, a member of Parliament and Minister of Tourism whose assassination this week prompted thirty Israeli tanks to rumble into historic Bethlehem in the middle of the night, firing left and right. The Palestinians claim that Zeevi's assassination was in retaliation for an Israeli assassination of one of their own, which, in turn, the Israelis claim was in retaliation for one of their own, which, in turn, the Palestinians claim was . . . well, you know how it goes. The latest link in this chain of infinite causation is the death of a twelve-year-old Palestinian sixth grader, who died when an errant shell struck her elementary school classroom. There is no end in sight to this chain, but there are always at least two accounts of its beginning.

Walking on the Tel Aviv beach, listening to music, seeing so many people of different nationalities play and coexist so peacefully, it's hard to comprehend the gruesome trauma unfolding only an hour or two away on any given day. Sometimes it seems like a form of denial or desensitization. More likely, it's a glimpse of what awaits in America's future: leaders encouraging their citizens to try to return to and maintain normal lives in the midst of an unpredictable environment of terrorism.

WEEK 4: ADJUSTMENTS

MY ONE-MONTH ANNIVERSARY! How time has flown.

University classes finally resumed this week, after the threat of a faculty strike was averted. Israeli faculty members tend to be underpaid relative to their American counterparts, and underpaid as well in comparison with local peers working in occupations of similar status. Many teach part-time in private colleges or develop consulting practices on the side to augment their income. This year, the faculty reportedly was seeking something in the ballpark of a 16 percent raise, while administration was countering with an offer of 6 percent. But in the end, the faculty agreed to at least start teaching and see what happens in negotiations later in the semester.

The Tel Aviv University campus is quite stunning. Built on the site of a former Arab village, it features a faculty club that once was the mansion of a sultan, an anachronistic reminder of a prior era. In front of the main gate is a broad, sweeping plaza ringed by white, contemporary buildings—a café, student center, and art gallery. Underfoot, paved squares paying homage to intellectual giants of the past offer quotes from Galileo and Newton, opening notes from a Beethoven Symphony, mathematical equations, and other important intellectual masterpieces. At the gate itself, a security guard checks every backpack, briefcase, and purse—causing lines at campus rush hour, as students and faculty alike wait to be searched. With the music school immediately adjacent, visitors are often greeted with strains of sopranos and pianos upon entering the grounds. Inside the gate, examples of ancient Roman columns line the right side of the sidewalk, while a contemporary sculpture garden borders the left. Heading up a few stairs, I reach my favorite sculpture on campus: a single piece of iron in the form of a rectangle. Elegant in its simplicity, it forms a frame through which one can see many beautiful and ever-changing sights: beautiful campus buildings in one direction, sculptures and flower gardens off on different angles, and glimpses of the Mediterranean Sea down at the end of Einstein Boulevard.

Remembering the past seems vitally important in Israel, and nowhere is this more evident than on university campuses. Just past the sculpture garden, I can sit on the Joshua and Sonia Bloch Family Terrace, which is connected to the Abraham and Edita Spiegel Family Building, which is connected to the Victor and Andrea Carter Building, which houses the Lady Sarah Cohen Exhibition Center and Susskind-Rokeach Hall (and lists the names of dozens of other donors), and which borders the David and Zipora Federmann Promenade. Virtually no building, garden, square, promenade, plaza, or sculpture is unnamed or unconnected to some historical or personal remembrance; with so many memorials, the past is freshly situated in the present, not just on campus but throughout the entire country as well.

My first class was a real learning experience—for me, at least, though I don't know what impact it had on the fourteen students who originally signed up. I was scheduled to teach "Mass Communication and Public Opinion" to upper-level undergraduates and beginning graduate students in Communication and allied departments in the social sciences. Warned ahead of time that Israeli students wouldn't read anything assigned, but would believe that they knew everything anyway, I pruned a lot of the readings from my syllabus to make it more compatible with student expectations, added a couple of new ones on Middle Eastern topics, spent hours attempting to craft an engaging course description and structure, and confidently strode into the classroom. It was at that point that, like Dorothy standing in Oz, I realized I wasn't in Kansas anymore. Like Americans heading to parties, Israeli students show up to class fashionably late, so only one student was present when I arrived sixty seconds before the scheduled start (having just left the first faculty meeting of the year down the hall). When the lone student realized that the class was being offered in English, she became the first casualty, fleeing the room as others started trickling in late. After introductions, I said that I expected them to actually read the assigned articles—and, more importantly, to do so *every week* instead of right before the exam. Two more immediately got up and left. Course requirements of one test *and* a five-page paper *and* a grade for class participation? That unfortunate news emptied another seat. Suddenly, with the ring of a cell phone, a fifth student got up and left the room for fifteen minutes, only to return in the middle of my course introduction to pick up her books and disappear out the door, never to be seen again. The final exit occurred a few minutes later, just as I was finally launching into my lecture. So, within a span of mere minutes, the original group of fourteen had suffered extensive collateral damage and was now pared to eight. One of the remaining students and a reassuring colleague told me not to worry, that students do these things all the time, that they're scared of classes taught in English, that they hate having to read regularly throughout the term, and that the ones who stay really want to be there. Time will tell, but in the meantime, I'm apparently doing my part to help control burgeoning enrollments at Tel Aviv U.

To commemorate surviving my first class, the next day I went with friends to a restaurant in which the waiters alternately sing on stage and wait on tables. The restaurant offers two 3-hour dinner shows each night, one starting at 9 P.M. for the early birds, the other starting at the more civilized hour of midnight (nightlife in Tel Aviv heats up well after things have cooled down in East Lansing). The singing was good, and through the Hebrew accents, I recognized familiar strains of Elton John, Barbara Streisand, and assorted rap artists. About two hours into the set, though, the place started getting wild. People danced on their chairs, up on the stage, on low walls separating tables, and in the aisles—wherever they could find a spare centimeter or two—while swinging to the tunes of lively traditional and contemporary Israeli songs. It was loud, raucous, and totally spontaneous. But what intrigued me the most was the mixture of ages in the room. The patrons represented a healthy cross-section of the spectrum, from sixty-something couples dancing arm-in-arm to rap, to twenty-something kids grooving to traditional party songs. There was a noticeable feeling of unity and spirit across generations that I don't usually see in the States. Young people didn't appear self-conscious or resentful of having to hang around elders or listen to occasional oldies, while adults didn't shake their heads in dismay at the new music or look disapprovingly at the unfamiliar dance steps of the young. Instead, everyone just did what they wanted where they wanted to do it, seemingly having a great time and reflecting a sense of real community in the process.

As I type the final lines of this report, an intriguing saga finally reaches its climax tonight with the long-awaited World Cup qualifying soccer match between Austria and Israel. In my story from Week 1, I noted that life had returned to normal in Tel Aviv and mentioned that the soccer match was going to be played that weekend as scheduled. As it turned out, the next day some members of the Austrian team refused to fly to Israel because of security concerns, and it appeared briefly as though the team would have to play short-handed. This triggered a volley of accusations and criticisms. Why didn't the Austrians want to come to Israel? Was there more to this than mere concern about terrorism and safety? A couple of days later, however, when a jet departing from Tel Aviv was shot down over the Black Sea, the game was officially postponed and rescheduled for tonight, a Saturday. Everything was on track until a new crisis emerged a couple of days ago: the Austrian team had reservations in a hotel that doesn't allow its kitchen staff to do any work on the Sabbath—including lighting matches for the gas stoves. It looked as though the team wouldn't be able to get a hot meal; and if the Austrians couldn't get a hot meal, they wouldn't come. This precipitated a new round of criticisms and accusations. Finally, the Israel Soccer Federation stepped in and made arrangements for the Austrians to get hot food delivered to their hotel. Tonight, the city came to a standstill while the match was in progress; in Israel, soccer has the combined stature of such Michigan favorites as football, basketball, hockey, and drinking beer. Bad news, though. The entire city deflated moments ago as the Austrians scored their only goal to tie the game with mere seconds left in penalty time, thereby moving on to play Turkey in the next round and leaving Israel out of the mix. It's a real shock to the locals, whose team was seconds away from advancing before losing to an adversary that hasn't exactly endeared itself to the population in recent weeks. The loss apparently broke the hearts of the gods as well, as for only the second time since last February, it is raining—really hard—in Tel Aviv. An omen! It wouldn't surprise me if the Austrians end up with only cold food after all in their hotel tonight . . .

WEEK 5: THE MEMORIAL

LAST WEEK, I DESCRIBED HOW my initial class meeting seemed to have more in common with a train station than a classroom: late arrivals, early departures, and the chirp of cell phones in the air. In contrast, this week—the first "real" class session following last week's introduction—was fabulous. The twelve students who appeared knew what the course was about, wanted to be there, and showed up on time. Best of all, they were intense and passionate, sophisticated in their knowledge of the political environment, and oblivious to our running past the normal closing hour. The palpable intensity of the discussion brought back fond memories of late-night discussions at the University of Wisconsin–Madison, where we would sit for hours and debate the merits of participatory democracy, or other subjects of comparable worth. Now, with my appetite whetted for more, classes are suddenly canceled with the launch of a faculty strike today. Nobody knows when classes will resume.

Last night, I attended the sixth annual memorial commemorating the assassination of Yitzhak Rabin. Rabin was a decorated warrior and commander of the military during the Six-Day War who eventually became the country's eleventh prime minister and a champion of peace. His efforts won him a shared Nobel Peace Prize (with Shimon Peres and Yasser Arafat), as well as the admiration and respect of many of his people. But certainly not all. Right-wing factions branded him a traitor and printed posters showing him dressed in a Nazi uniform and wearing an Arab headdress. In the days leading to his assassination, his minister of the environment was forced off the road, while his minister of education was punched in the stomach. Then, on that fateful eve of November 4, 1995, Rabin addressed a huge rally and thanked those in attendance for their commitment to the peace process. Moments later, while heading to the parking lot, he was shot and killed by Yigal Amir, a young Israeli law student at Bar-Ilan University. How could such a thing happen so publicly? Was there a conspiracy? Why did the Shin Bet secret service fall down on the job? In a sense, Israeli security seemed blinded by the same in-the-box thinking as our FBI and CIA on September 11: preoccupied with external threats, the security forces never imagined an attack would come from within—and, in this case, from one of their own. Amir, disenchanted with the direction that the peace process was taking, believed that someone had to put an end to it. Many here believe that by assassinating Rabin, he did just that.

Every Friday afternoon in what is now Rabin Square, small groups have held vigils commemorating the event. And each year, a memorial service is organized, last night being the sixth. Security was tight—about as tight as I would expect if George Bush decided to visit Kabul, Afghanistan, and address the Rotary Club. Hours before the rally, soldiers and police set up barricades several blocks away from Rabin Square. Large city buses were parked sideways on the boulevards leading to the square, forming impenetrable barriers to would-be suicide drivers. Bands of armed soldiers roamed the streets, testing cars and trash receptacles for explosives. Overhead, a large blimp provided surveillance of the downtown area, a helicopter circled, and armed police crouched on the rooftops of nearby buildings, searching for the first sign of trouble. People young and old streamed into the square, but only after passing through inspection and x-ray of bags and backpacks. Plainclothes police roamed through the crowd, players in a vigil of anticipated violence during a memorial service for peace. Who, I asked, would commit violence on a night like tonight? The answer was offered with a certain air of resignation and sadness: violence at the rally, people thought, could just as likely be the work of fellow citizens on the political Right as of Palestinian terrorists.

In a car sitting in traffic outside the barricades, an animated Israeli man cursed the rally and those attending, clearly agitated at the sight of the growing crowd. Hundreds of youths were now marching down the streets, many wearing uniforms and carrying banners in support of peace. Groups staked out their territory throughout the square. Near the back stood the resolute "Women in Black"—no, not advance publicity for some Geena Davis sequel to a Tommie Lee Jones sci-fi flick, but rather a political movement of men as well as women dedicated to peace. In the middle were packs of blue-shirted members of the youth movement. Those with red laces in their shirts were part of the "Working-Learning Group," while the ones with white laces were members of the "Young Guard." Nearby were uniformed members of various scouting troops—akin to American Boy and Girl Scouts. Followers of Meretz mingled through the crowd, hoping to recruit new supporters to the party, while "Peace

Now" workers sold T-shirts in a booth. Belgian youths, marching and singing, carried placards showing Israeli and Palestinian flags combined in unity. And scattered randomly throughout were the most poignant participants of all: the candle children, who sat on the ground in circles and arrayed lit candles in the shape of the sixties' U.S. peace symbol, thereby continuing a ritual started by their older brothers and sisters during the initial memorial service in 1995. Thousands of others attended as well; three different newspapers today offered crowd estimates of sixty thousand, eighty thousand, and one hundred thousand. While it seems like a lot of people, many to whom I spoke were disappointed by the turnout. The political Left appears to be getting tired and losing momentum with every new report of a suicide bomb or assassination.

Overall, the service seemed to lack a certain focus, as people milled about, seemingly waiting for some inspirational speech or galvanizing gesture. But noticeably absent, for a change, were politicians. Why? The popular belief is that the organizers did not want to invite Prime Minister Sharon, and the most palatable way of achieving this was to simply declare the rally off-limits to all politicians (though the mayor of Tel Aviv did at least greet attendees). Nevertheless, some of the live music was indeed very inspirational. Several years ago, Al Gore read Walt Whitman's poem "O Captain, My Captain" at Rabin's memorial service in the States, linking Rabin's assassination to that of Abraham Lincoln (in whose memory the poem was originally written). The poem, translated into Hebrew, was set to beautiful music and performed last night, and now is one of several songs linked in a special manner with the late prime minister.

Fortunately, no violence erupted, and the rally ended without incident. Today, however, is a different matter. Reports from nearby Jerusalem tell of a Palestinian gunman who sprayed a city bus with gunfire, killing two and wounding fifty. Rabin's hope of peace, tantalizingly close six short years ago, today looms as a distant mirage.

WEEK 6: MONEY

QUESTION: HOW CAN YOU end up with a small fortune in Israel?

Answer: Come here with a large one.

Tel Aviv is supposedly the fifth most expensive city in the world, and it lives up to its reputation in many large and small ways. A small plastic bottle of orange juice costs nearly twice as much as in the famous citrus state of Michigan; an issue of an English-language newspaper purchased on the streets costs between $1.50 and $2.00. If I go to the cleaners, I feel like I've been taken to the cleaners, so I instead wash my shirts and hang them out to dry (inside out, as the intense Mediterranean sun has an alchemist's ability to convert MSU green into MSU white). But I have picked up one expensive vice: I'll often stop at one of the hundreds of small, open-air stands and plop down $2.00 for a 100-gram sack of warm cashews or almonds on the way to the bus stop. Bus service, by the way, is a rare bargain, both efficient and affordable, with an added bonus that the drivers are even trained to defuse bombs.

Going to the grocery store is one of the more stressful events of my week, and I try to avoid it like the plague. First, it is expensive. Second, it is a crowded and chaotic contact sport. In a single short, narrow aisle, I've stood and watched while more than twenty shoppers jockey, clash, and crash their carts for position in a roller derby of frozen foods. Third, since I don't read or speak Hebrew, I rarely know what I am *really* buying until I get home and open it up, and even then I'm only half sure. The seated check-out clerks appear to be Israel's version of bored American airport security staff, though not nearly as friendly. And the self-service plastic bags seem to be glued shut, often spoiling my attempts at a quick getaway. On the other hand, I have reached some modicum of peace with aspects of grocery shopping. The fresh fruits and vegetables look the same in Hebrew as in English, so they are fairly predictable purchases. Ten-packs of frozen microwavable pizzas and Canadian granola have become my staples. And the deli counter clerks are especially tolerant souls. When they ask me how much sliced turkey I want (at least that's what I think they're asking), I'll make a few gestures with my fingers, squint my eyes, and shake my head; they'll do the same, and pretty soon we've reached a beautiful (nonverbal) understanding.

Other than food, where does the money go? The real money trail starts with taxes. Your average middle-class wage earners lose about 50 percent of their salary right off the top to income taxes. Next, add to that a "steep" health insurance tax, an "onerous" real estate tax, and the topper: a 17 percent Value Added Tax applied to pretty much every product or service purchased (including even Internet access just to send these notes!). Buying a car? There's reportedly a tariff of around 100 percent on imported automobiles, meaning that your basic $20,000 Chevy in Lansing starts at around $40,000 here. There is significant competition between brands, with greater diversity of European and Japanese cars here than in the States, but less competition within brands. If you want a Chevy in Israel, you pretty much have only one choice for a dealer, so many of the familiar U.S. bargaining tricks of the trade simply won't work here.

From taxes, the trail leads to housing. Housing costs in downtown Tel Aviv, as in most cities in the world, can be exorbitant or affordable depending upon location and number of rooms. While a two-bedroom flat in a modest downtown building might range from $200,000 to $300,000 (less in South Tel Aviv), a more desirable four-bedroom flat in a newer tower nearer the beach might approach, if not exceed, $1 million. Worse yet, buyers are expected to make a down payment of at least 50 percent, meaning that flats tend to be passed down from one generation to the next, thereby limiting the potential for social mobility to some degree.

Where else does the money go? People definitely splurge on high culture. Tel Aviv is a world-class center of the arts, and opportunities abound to hear great music. On many blocks in the downtown area you can find musicians, usually Russians, who sit and play their hearts out in the hopes of attracting a spare shekel or two. If they could, they'd play in one of the excellent local symphonies, but the supply of qualified musicians— and singers, actors, and performers of all types—is simply too great. Russians do indeed love their music—especially opera, for which they turn out in full force and in elegant attire. Before a recent performance, several approached me in the hopes that I was a ticket scalper. East Lansing may have its football, but in Tel Aviv a different cultural form stirs the passions and opens the wallets.

So far, I've enjoyed a stirring performance of Vivaldi's *Gloria*, managed to remain awake watching the famous Swiss mimes

"The Mummenschanz," and purchased tickets for a light evening of Mendelssohn and a heavy rendition of *La Traviata*. And this doesn't even include the recent Oud Days Festival in Jerusalem, religious music festivals in Abu Ghosh, or the upcoming Tel Aviv–Jaffa Festival, which features Spanish dancers, Greek vocalists, Irish bands, New York jazz, and a prominent Czech gypsy singer. Throw in a vibrant theater community, and countless nightclubs and cafés featuring Israeli or European bands, and you have incredible entertainment possibilities (made even more amazing by the fact that this is a period of somewhat diminished opportunities, due to terrorism and some canceled performances). But none of it is cheap.

A lot of people's money seems to end up in the coffers of telecommunications firms as well. Everywhere I go, I see men and women wearing what I call the "Tel Aviv earring," otherwise known as the cell phone, hanging from people's ears (reminds me of the old Simon and Garfunkel song, "The Dangling Conversation"). Cell phone penetration is among the highest in the world, and life here might come to a screeching halt if people didn't have twenty-four-hour access to each other. As a hardcore resister of this technology, I have no idea of the attraction of this uncompromising electronic tether. The most interesting sight, though, has to be that occasional group of three or four people sitting together in a café, each forsaking the immediacy of communication with each other for a private chat with someone who isn't there.

In one final quest to get a better handle on where people spend their money, I thought it might be enlightening to consult the English-language version of the Yellow Pages. The pages are on smaller sheets of paper than in the States, so at best this exercise can only provide some relative sense of spending opportunities and priorities (or beliefs about English-speaking

34

visitors' priorities). Let's see . . . there are six pages of listings for air conditioning (totally understandable), ten pages of hair stylists and another five for beauticians, one page of circumcisers (hmm . . . a category presumably "cut" from the East Lansing directory), six pages of diamonds (Tel Aviv is a global center for this industry), two pages just for carburetors (must be all that sand in the air), nine pages of fashion houses, two pages of yeshivas, and *forty-one* (yes, 41) *pages* of listings for lawyers! *Finally!* Now it's completely clear why Tel Aviv is such an expensive city in which to live . . .

WEEK 7: THE OLD CITY

IN SEARCH OF MY TEL AVIV "Cheers"—that friendly little place where I am a regular and everybody knows my name. The other night, I tried a promising prospect: a crowded café overlooking the water on the northern section of the beach in the Old Harbor. Pleasant surroundings, friendly people, and a waiter who was trying really hard to say all the right things in his non-native tongue. I was feeling pretty confident when I ordered the "fried fish," thinking that it would probably resemble Bennigan's fish and chips, with just a touch of Mediterranean pizzazz. Much to my, uh, surprise, a waiter set in front of me a plate holding a large, dead fish—fins, tail, and eyes intact—that had been gutted and tossed in a deep-fat fryer. Yup, definitely fried fish alright; no truth-in-advertising problem here. I sure didn't have to worry that they were trying to fool me by serving me cat or chicken instead. I calmly and casually glanced around the room a couple of times with a pleasant look pasted on my face, took a couple of moments to survey the scene in front of me, and then discreetly dragged a small piece of lettuce across the plate to cover the fish's eye before impaling the beast with my fork. It actually tasted much better than it looked, once again reinforcing the old adage that you can't judge a fish by its (crispy fried) scales.

The next day, I headed to Jerusalem for a meeting with officials from a governmental ministry. With time to kill before a late-afternoon meeting, I wandered around Jerusalem, soaking up the sights and sounds. My meanderings first took me to Mea She'arim, a neighborhood where ultra-Orthodox Jews live and study. Plastered to the walls of buildings and hanging prominently over the streets were bright warning signs—in English as well as Hebrew—imploring women and girls not to enter unless they were dressed in proper attire: no pants, no tight clothing, no dresses above the knees. Tour groups were told to stay out as well, as a sign of respect for the neighborhood, its religious beliefs, and the education of its children. I later heard from friends that driving through the neighborhood on Saturday, the day of rest, has been known to elicit a hailstorm of stones and dirty diapers from the residents. My own trek through the neighborhood was uneventful, though as I left, I thought about the irony that it was a woman soldier—wearing pants—who put a deadly end to the most recent terrorist attack in downtown Jerusalem. A terrorist had just sprayed a city bus with automatic gunfire, killing several passengers and wounding fifty more, but the woman soldier shot and killed him before he could do even more damage. Having risked her life to save her fellow citizens, she was a hero of the city, yet she wouldn't be welcome here if wearing pants.

I next headed down the hill to the Old City, the epicenter of tension and violence in the Middle East, and home to some of the most cherished locales and legends of Islam, Judaism, and Christianity. A number of Israelis with whom I spoke said they won't go in the Old City to shop in the Arab booths because of recent bombings, shootings, and stabbings. They didn't know if the City was still frequented by tourists or deserted, but I figured that, as a non-Israeli, I'd be safe—especially if merchants wanted to attract future tourists and their dollars. Though I wasn't wearing a "God Bless America" cap, American flag lapel pin, or "I ♥ NY" emblem, I nonetheless felt ready to proceed. To enter the City from where I was, I had to walk down a very narrow stone sidewalk, hemmed in by buildings and closed doorways on the left and a bank of cars and large buses on the right. My pace quickened, and I started feeling a bit claustrophobic as I was swallowed up in a large crowd of Arabs headed in the same direction. Like a fish in a school, I had been swept up in a vortex with a direction and momentum all its own, and couldn't go my own way if I tried. As we reached a wide boulevard and the crowd thinned, I noticed dozens of young Arab men sitting around aimlessly, talking and smoking, apparently having nowhere to work or nothing to do in the middle of the afternoon. I entered through Damascus Gate, the arched and decorative entrance that once welcomed visiting emperors and kings. I didn't see anyone else who resembled a tourist in this particular quarter, just Arabs going about their business of buying and selling their wares. The unexpected sight of a small lad wearing a familiar maize and blue University of Michigan T-shirt was a jarring but oddly comforting reminder of my world thousands of miles away, though in any other setting this symbol of MSU's arch rival would have elicited a totally different reaction. The sight of three Israeli soldiers wearing bullet-proof vests and carrying automatic rifles was reassuring as well, but for very different reasons. I wandered aimlessly, ever conscious of bodies careening toward me from all directions in the crowded and narrow passages, before heading out and starting the trek back up the hill, this time to Jaffa Road.

When I made it to the top, I noticed four large crowds of people, each standing on one of four street corners more than a block apart. More surprising yet, the people were quiet, an amazing occurrence in and of itself, and appeared to be looking at the same scene. The road itself was closed down, and a tall, bulky Israeli soldier stood in the middle, facing in my direction, brandishing his rifle and resembling some modern-day Colossus. Behind him were three police vans arranged in a semi-circle in front of a bus stop. It seems that a suspicious bag had been left at the stop, and now a small robot was picking it up and shaking it. This time it was just an innocent package, and soon the police rode off and the crowds dispersed. A local shop clerk told me that such things happen "every day now," and added that the police have become very proficient at handling these situations. Israelis are used to this, he said, but it is still new to the Americans.

From Jaffa Road, I headed to the Gabriel Sherover Promenade and drove along a magnificent roadway overlooking a valley and several parks, with a stunning view of the Old City. My meeting was at the Taverna Restaurant, located in a serene, though windy and cool setting on the hillside. As is my custom, I ordered my salad plain; but a few moments later, the waitress returned and said that the chef didn't want to serve my salad plain, because his dressing was so good. Hmmm . . . Since he was about to prepare the rest of my order, and I had no way of gauging his potential for passive-aggressiveness, I thought it prudent to compromise, and the salad promptly appeared with dressing on the side. The seafood entrée, by the way, was exquisitely prepared and needed no garnish of a lettuce eye-patch.

Later in the afternoon, I left the time warp that is Jerusalem, a city solidly rooted in ancient tradition, and headed westward toward contemporary Tel Aviv, a city making it up as it goes along, silhouetted in a blazing red sun setting on the Mediterranean. Somewhere in between, the mood among passengers in the car changed from heaviness and somberness to light-heartedness and relief, as we got farther and farther from Jerusalem. Though I've previously spent time in both Ann Arbor and East Lansing, it is still nevertheless quite remarkable how two cities separated by mere kilometers in distance can feel light-years apart in atmosphere.

WEEK 8: CONFLICTS

AUTUMN ARRIVED ABRUPTLY this week with the howl of cool winds, and with it came some inevitable modifications to the comfortable Tel Aviv lifestyle. One morning, waking up to this new and unwelcome season without a blanket, I shivered, stumbled out of bed onto a cold tile floor, and headed to the thermostat to get some heat going. Of course, there is no thermostat—or heat of any kind—in the apartment, as these older Tel Aviv flats were built to compensate for long, hot summers rather than short, cool winters. So I decided to take a warm shower. Of course, there is no hot water unless I first turn on the hot water heater and leave it running for about twenty minutes. So I decided it must be time to shop for warmer clothes. No problems there. At the nearby mall on Ibn Gvirol, I marveled at the seemingly endless diversity of men's designer labels in this city of European-style fashion elegance, far more than one could hope to find in even the most comprehensive Farm and Fleet superstore in central Michigan. On the streets, the change in season is more noticeable in the outfits of the women than the men. During most of the year, the most popular women's fashion statement by far—at least among women under the age of seventy or so—is the bare midriff. With the chill of fall in the air, though, this style is giving way to a slightly more covered look—though nothing remotely approaching Taliban standards.

Much of the attention in the academic world this past week focused on the three-week-long faculty strike at universities throughout the country, which was supposed to end yesterday but still lingers. An e-mail to faculty reporting the latest details of the negotiations ended with the sobering comment that "After the dust clears, we must start a true analysis, without hiding anything, of the grave failure we have been steeped in. A real lesson should be learned." I would wholeheartedly agree with that assessment. While the faculty's grievances were indisputably legitimate—Israeli faculty are severely underpaid by any standard of comparison—the strike itself was a public relations nightmare. First, it unsuccessfully tried to compete for limited attention (and dollars) with simultaneous strikes by firefighters, the National Insurance Institute, Labor and Social Affairs Ministry, Customs and VAT office, the Land Registry—and even a strike at Ben Gurion Airport. Several of these competing strikes had direct and dire consequences for many citizens' businesses and livelihoods, thus automatically relegating the faculty strike to a position of lesser prominence. Second, the faculty's publicity efforts were meager, compounding the position of competitive disadvantage. It's as though the faculty organized an elaborate party, but forgot to invite anyone. Third, the threat of the faculty strike seemed to pale in comparison to national concerns about the economy, unemployment, and terrorism, and so the strikers neither won friends nor influenced people. Fourth, the strike didn't appear to be very popular with portions of the faculty, either. And fifth, the strike was just terribly confusing. Only classes taught by the "senior" faculty were affected, leaving some classes still offered, others canceled, and students forced to figure out the difference.

The strike took an odd turn of events this week when students joined the fray, protesting the effects of the strikes on their academic progress. At Ben Gurion University, students reportedly used camels to block entrances to the university. At the Technion, students practiced their engineering and communication skills, respectively, by building a cinderblock wall around the entrance and getting into shouting matches with faculty attempting to cross the line. At Tel Aviv University, about twenty student demonstrators sealed the main entrance to the university with a padlock and chain. The students were very media-savvy and soon attracted a crowd of reporters nearly as large as their own group. One student told me that she and her fellow demonstrators felt obligated to "help" the faculty because they were making so little progress. Thoughtful students. At the very least, they drew more media attention in fifteen minutes than their faculty mentors had in two weeks. And the most delicious part of all was that, in their preoccupation with faithfully documenting every minute detail of this completely symbolic event at the main gate, the reporters either failed to notice or perhaps simply chose to ignore dozens of faculty and students carrying on business as usual, entering and exiting the university at a gate just around the corner.

The American holiday of Thanksgiving came and went this week without any fanfare. With no classes to teach or holidays to celebrate, I had extra opportunities to sample local culture. Theaters are abundant and offer quite a diverse selection of films from Europe and the Middle East, as well as the usual fare from America. My Thanksgiving was spent at the home of the

American Zionist Organization, watching the Iranian film *Kandahar*, a film with a timely title but disappointing script that nevertheless offers an amazing glimpse of how Afghan people have suffered from fundamentalist control and deadly land mines. Earlier in the week, a much more engaging Iranian film, *The Color of Paradise*, told the sad but inspiring story of a boy who is blind and a father who doesn't want him in his home. Having been weaned on the story-book Hollywood cinematic diet, I found these films disconcerting and remarkable for their routine, realistic, and unflinching depictions of human suffering. No gimmicks, soft edges, or contrivances here: just straightforward accounts of ordinary human beings in prosaic surroundings, confronting the tragedies and joys of their worlds. *Divorce Iranian Style* will complete my Iranian trilogy in the coming week.

A serendipitous opportunity to experience some local culture also presented itself this week when followers of a deceased rabbi (Rabbi Nachman of Breslau) passed my flat late one night. It seems that these young men like to drive down the streets of Tel Aviv at night, blasting their lively music, and getting out of the car to dance periodically when stopped at a red light. Why do they do this? They are missionaries, using music to attract attention to their cause of taming godless Tel Aviv. An irate neighbor yelled to them to be quiet, and later described what she saw as a double standard: if *she* went into *their* neighborhood and blasted her music at midnight, she said, they would stone her car, but they know that they can blast away with impunity in the secular neighborhoods. All I know is that while I can personally attest to the success of the missionaries' attempts to attract attention, I remain unconvinced of any additional proselytizing benefits of this particular campaign strategy.

The main professional accomplishment of my week was to give the keynote address to more than three hundred attendees at this year's edition of the National Conference on Health Education and Health Promotion, sponsored by the Ministry of Health. It went extraordinarily well: one of those gratifying talks in which everything seems to click. Some amusing videotapes, anecdotes, and excellent translator's commentary helped, but much of the credit has to go to a colleague who spent seven hours translating my PowerPoint slides into Hebrew, something that few invited American speakers are in a position to do. At least forty attendees made a point of approaching me and offering their heartfelt thanks for my presentation, with most inviting me to give follow-up talks at their organizations as well. If I didn't have other responsibilities to fulfill, I could easily spend the rest of my time here giving lectures and workshops throughout the country. One particularly touching compliment came from a sincere young Arab student, who told me in halting English that I would be his family's honored guest if I could arrange to visit his village during my stay here in Israel. It was a moving gesture on his part, one of many that I enjoyed this day from this warm, vibrant, and dedicated public health community.

WEEK 9: VIOLENCE

Preface*

I had just finished the following report, and was about to hit the "send" button, when news broke Saturday night of the horrifying suicide bombings in Jerusalem, followed the next day by news of an equally horrifying suicide bombing in Haifa. What follows is my original report, coincidentally written to give an idea of the ongoing

*EDITORIAL NOTE: This is the only letter for which I felt compelled to include a preface and conclusion. When I reread what I had written, it appeared as though my letter could be viewed as an attempt to provide a context for, and hence an understanding of, the events that led to the bombing. Though this was not my intention (I had written this letter well before the news of the bombing), I suddenly understood one of the major shortcomings of journalism. Through its emphasis on facts and reporting discrete events, journalism reports incidents in a contextual vacuum, presumably letting the reader make the relevant historical, political, economic, and cultural associations. When reporters do provide context, they are usually criticized for being biased, as no single person can provide every possible perspective on any given event, especially in a medium with severe constraints on space. Further, in the realm of reporting on terrorism, providing context is often viewed as providing understanding, which is equated with providing justification for an action. This is considered outrageous to victims of terrorism who (a) have no desire to share even partial responsibility for a terrorist's actions and (b) do not want others to feel sympathy (resulting from understanding what drove him or her to commit such an act) for a man or woman engaging in terrorism. Knowing this, I found myself in a bizarre quandary of being on a mission to enhance understanding of a culture, while not wanting to appear as though I was attempting to enhance understanding of a specific event in that same culture. I found this to be a difficult tightrope to walk and hence added this preface.

violence outside of Tel Aviv. Because many of these incidents are considered "routine" violence and hence "not newsworthy" beyond the local area, few probably made their way into the pages of small-town American newspapers. I had read the local paper every day during this one-week period, but the sheer volume of carnage didn't register with me until I sat down and listed all the deaths and attacks for this report, which was a bit numbing to do. The information is drawn from news accounts in the English-language version of *Ha'aretz*, a leading, though limited in circulation, Israeli newspaper, and major international news websites.

IN THE DAYS PRECEDING November 22, American Thanksgiving, things had been pretty calm here. Israeli Prime Minister Sharon repeatedly has stated that peace negotiations could begin only following seven days of peace, and both sides appeared to be engaging in restraint. American envoy Anthony Zinni would be arriving in a few days, and everyone seemed eager to make a good impression.

Back in America, families were preparing to sit down to the traditional dinner of turkey and pumpkin pie. And while residents of Tel Aviv were wrapping up another routine week of work, all hell seemed to be breaking loose everywhere else.

• • •

THURSDAY, NOVEMBER 22

Five Palestinian boys, ages seven to fourteen, living in the Khan Yunis refugee camp, were blown up while walking to their elementary school. Palestinians were horrified, and called for investigations. Israeli military authorities first speculated that the children were killed by Palestinian bomb materials, then that they were killed while kicking an unexploded Israeli tank shell. Two days later, they admitted that they had planted a bomb to kill Palestinian snipers who had been firing on nearby Jewish settlements, and speculated that the children must have triggered it instead.

FRIDAY, NOVEMBER 23

Following an emotional funeral for the five children, angry Palestinian youths marched near the Gush Katif Jewish settlements, vowing revenge and throwing rocks at the fence surrounding the enclave. Israeli soldiers fired tear gas, and shot and killed a fifteen-year-old Palestinian demonstrator. Israeli soldiers shot and killed a Palestinian taxi driver, and wounded two of his seven passengers near Rafah. The army said it had received prior warnings about plans to plant a car bomb near the base. When the taxi had twice approached an army post after dark and was approaching for a third time, soldiers opened fire, fearing that the car contained attackers. The passengers said the driver was just lost. Two Palestinians died in a blast in Beit Iba, either from an Israeli bomb or while attempting to plant their own bomb on a road frequented by Israeli motorists. Israeli soldiers in helicopters fired missiles at a van and killed three men believed to be members of the terrorist group Hamas. Israeli leaders were relieved, if not ecstatic upon confirming that they had killed the number one terrorist on Israel's "Most Wanted" list, reacting as American leaders might to the news of Osama bin Laden's death at the hands of American troops in Afghanistan. In contrast, some twenty thousand Palestinians mourned the deaths of the three men—and the nine other

Palestinians who had also died violent deaths in the preceding twenty-four hours—in a large public funeral in Gaza. Some in attendance vowed that revenge would soon come in Tel Aviv.

Saturday, November 24

Palestinians fired mortar rounds into a military base near the Jewish settlement of Kfar Darom, killing one reserve soldier and injuring two others. Palestinians fired a mortar shell into the Jewish settlement of Gush Katif, damaging a house and the room of a one-year-old infant, who was unharmed. Palestinians fired into the southern Jerusalem neighborhood of Gilo and into the Jewish settlement of Dugit, each with no apparent casualties.

Sunday, November 25

Israeli military helicopters fired missiles at a Palestinian military intelligence office in Khan Yunis and at a Palestinian naval position in Soudaniyeh, wounding several. Palestinians fired mortars into the Jewish settlement of Netzarim and at Israeli military outposts in Gush Katif and Rafah, wounding two soldiers. Israeli soldiers shot and killed a fourteen-year-old Palestinian girl when they opened fire at demonstrators in the West Bank. Palestinians wounded an Israeli woman by throwing stones at her car near Halhul. Israeli soldiers near Bethlehem shot and killed a thirteen-year-old Palestinian boy who was attempting to throw a Molotov cocktail at them. South of Hebron, a roadside bomb exploded near a six-car convoy carrying Israel's chief of staff and several generals. No injuries were reported.

MONDAY, NOVEMBER 26

A Palestinian bomber blew himself up and wounded two policemen in Gaza. Palestinians fired into the Jerusalem neighborhood of Gilo, with no casualties reported. American envoy Anthony Zinni arrived in hopes of bringing peace to the Middle East.

TUESDAY, NOVEMBER 27

Two Palestinian gunmen slipped into Afula in a stolen car with Israeli plates, shot and killed two Israelis, and wounded fourteen others. Police and reserve soldiers killed the gunmen. A Palestinian fired at Israeli cars in Gush Katif, killing one woman and wounding three other people before being killed by Israeli military. Israeli military either wounded or killed a Palestinian man near Khan Yunis. Palestinians wounded a Thai citizen who was driving his car near Ma'aleh Levona.

WEDNESDAY, NOVEMBER 28

Shootings occurred in Gilo, Nisanit, Homesh, Har Grizam, Yad Yair, Kafr, Erez, Neveh Dekalim, and Rafah, but no injuries were reported. Israeli military either wounded or killed a Palestinian man near a border point. An Israeli motorist ran over and killed an elderly Palestinian man near Nablus. Palestinians said the action was intentional; Israeli police said it was an accident.

THURSDAY, NOVEMBER 29

A Palestinian bomber blew himself up along with three Israelis on a bus headed for Tel Aviv from Nazareth. The blast, which ripped apart the bus, wounded nine others, including motorists in nearby cars. Palestinian gunmen in Baka a-Sharkiya shot at Israeli soldiers, killing one and injuring another before escaping in a car. At the Bega'ot junction, Israeli military shot and killed a Palestinian who fled in his car after refusing to stop and get out as ordered. A Palestinian taxi driver sitting nearby was killed inadvertently by the Israeli gunfire.

. . .

Approximately thirty violent deaths and many more injuries in a single week of shootings and bombings, Thursday to Thursday (two days before the most recent suicide bombing in Jerusalem). It's terribly sad. Each death cannot adequately be understood through a mere sentence or with mention of a name or number, but rather must be viewed in terms of an irrevocable and senseless loss—of someone's friend, loved one, dreams, potential, innocence, tolerance, and trust. In my university class, which finally resumed on Thursday after a three-week strike, our discussions naturally gravitated to these events. One student described her own reactions by saying that when she read her first news story about a suicide bombing several years ago, she cried and couldn't even finish reading the article. Now, she can and does regularly finish news stories about much worse. The threshold for shock seemingly gets raised weekly with every fresh report of a shooting or suicide bombing, and the only way to cope is to emotionally detach. It isn't really denial; everyone is aware of the violence. But people are resolved not to be paralyzed or to give up, and so life goes on as normal, with the sobering awareness that anything can happen anywhere, and nothing can be done to prevent it.

WEEK 10: HOPE

THE SHORT, SLENDER MAN in green military
fatigues paced nervously as he puffed on his cigarette. He
looked suspiciously out of place with his moustache, black sub-
machine gun, and bulging duffle bag at this downtown Tel Aviv
bus stop—otherwise populated with women and clean-shaven
men heading to offices or schools. What was in the bag, and
why was he so nervous? Was he really an Israeli soldier, or
merely a terrorist masquerading as one (as happened a couple
of weeks ago)? I dismissed my thoughts as the bus he boarded
disappeared into thick traffic without incident. Now aboard the
No. 25, I notice for the first time how close our bus is to unfamiliar trucks, vans, and parked cars on these narrow streets.
It really wouldn't take much to start an explosive chain
reaction . . .

Why was I thinking like this? It had to be the inevitable by-
product of being immersed in reports about the latest wave of
suicide bombings in Jerusalem and Haifa, similar to Americans'
reactions to airplanes upon awakening on the morning of

September 12. People are on edge here. The U.S. State Department is again advising Americans to defer travel to Israel; Americans already in Israel should exercise "extreme caution," while staying away from restaurants, shopping malls, and bus stops. But, of course, that's nearly impossible to do.

In the days immediately following the bombings, Tel Aviv streets and cafés were largely deserted. No doubt some people avoided public places in order to be safe; but a friend explained that people might also be feeling guilty about appearing to have fun during a period of sadness. Plus, torrential rains were soaking the entire country—rains so severe that two people drowned. The deluge added to the somber mood, but at least offered a brief and much-needed respite between old, new, and retaliatory acts of violence. It was during one of these downpours that I sat and drank tea with one of my favorite new friends in all of Tel Aviv—my landlady, Hannah.

In her mid-eighties, Hannah is strong of will, keen of wit, and sharp as a tack, blessed with a phenomenal memory for detail from her youth. She is also slowly dying from brain cancer, but totally at peace with her world. She has lived on this same street for sixty-eight years and has, in her own words, enjoyed a full life of friendship, love, and the special joy that only twelve great-grandchildren can bring. Though Hannah is very sad about the violence this morning, she is less fatalistic than most. She starts telling me the story of her grandson, Dror, who was a mere nine years of age when he wrote a letter to God during the 1973 War, and translates a portion of it into English for me:

> Dear God of Heaven and Earth: Children in our neighborhood don't understand what is going on. We wait for salvation. People talk about peace, people meet and say "shalom"

and sing songs about peace, and yet we are always at war. Newspapers show pictures of wounded soldiers, crying mothers, upset children. And you let the Nazis kill six million of us. That's why we decided to write. If you really care, why don't you stop the wars and bring us peace?

—(signed) Dror, and the children of the neighborhood

Touched by the letter, Hannah, who does not consider herself particularly religious, asked Dror several weeks later if he had heard back from God. He hadn't, but added that he understood, saying that God was undoubtedly very busy with all that was going on. A few weeks later, though, he told his grandmother that he himself had written his own reply to share with his neighborhood friends who were awaiting God's answer. It went something like this:

Dear Dror and children of the neighborhood: I was very pleased to receive your letter. I have suffered, too, with you when good people and mothers and children were killed in the war; I cried too. But believe me, children, I tried more than once to go down and make peace in the world, but each time I arrived on your doorsteps I heard fighting inside. No one heard me, and I came back very sad. If you really want peace, begin at home with your family, your brothers and sisters, your friends, your neighbors, and even neighboring groups of people. Then peace will come.

—(signed) God of Heaven and Earth

Hannah smiled and brushed a tear from her eye when she finished reading Dror's letters. Clearly, if her grandson possessed this kind of wisdom at nine years of age, the peace that had eluded her generation would surely be realized in the future.

Listening to her faith in the younger generations, I couldn't help but feel inspired by her conviction and optimism.

Every winter has its spring, and even periods of death and despair are offset by eras of rebirth and hope. The morning after the suicide bombing in Jerusalem, St. Anthony's Catholic Church in Jaffa was bustling. Here it was two hours before the scheduled African Mass, and volunteers were already out in full force, decorating the entrance with blue and white streamers and garlands, and a sign reading "Grace Weds Ike."

But the wedding was still a long way off. The first order of business was the baptism of two babies—one a Filipino girl named Kim, the other a Nigerian boy named Henry. The American priest delegated readings to members of both families, sprinkled the babies with holy water, and even added a prayer of exorcism to rid the two of any evil spirits that might have descended upon them as a result of a family curse, evil eye, or cultural hex. After the two sets of parents and accompanying godparents agreed to raise their children in the Church, the ceremony ended, and the happy families headed outside for a round of photos before the start of the eleven o'clock mass.

The Filipino and Nigerian families were part of a large service class here in Tel Aviv: mostly maids, caretakers for the elderly, agricultural workers, laborers. They generally make very little money, but appear to take their religion quite seriously. Women appear in beautiful robes from their homelands, men wear suits, and even little children strut up and down the aisles wearing jackets and ties. (To fully appreciate the significance of this, you would have to know that Israeli attire is in general quite casual, and in any given year, many men never even wear a tie.) The Filipinos and Nigerians are not the only ethnic Christians that diligently attend mass at St. Anthony's and St. Peter's—the only two Catholic churches in the Tel Aviv–Jaffa area. Between the two, mass is offered in English, Hebrew, Romanian, Arabic, Italian, Spanish, and Polish. But the African Mass is the most interesting. This service is so popular that latecomers will not find an open pew, and must instead sit and kneel on the uncomfortable stone floor in the back of the church—which, by the way, they willingly do.

The procession begins with about twenty men walking up the aisle in pairs, followed by the choir of sixteen singers—dressed in robes that match the colors of each liturgical season and carrying African drums. The priest and his assistants follow, and finally the large wedding party appears. The wedding ceremony itself is quite simple, with the congregation breaking out in applause each time Grace or Ike recites a set of vows. But what really makes the service is the music. The choir is fantastic and gets the entire congregation—including the priest—swaying to the rhythmic beat of the drums and singing. In most churches back home, one or two parishioners participate in the Offertory service by carrying the collected donations up to the altar. Not at the African Mass in Jaffa. Here, as the choir sings lively, up-tempo songs, approximately one hundred parishioners sway and dance in obvious delight on their way to the altar, carrying twelve-packs of Sprite and Coca-Cola, containers of bottled water, sacks of grain—and, of course, the collected donations as well. It is an extraordinary spectacle of sight and sound, still more evidence that even in the unpredictable swirl of violence and hatred, life goes on, new seeds of optimism are sown, and new generations are born to promises and hopes of peace.

WEEK 11: GOING NATIVE

AS I WRITE THIS LETTER, Hanukkah is in full swing here in Tel Aviv, opening up all kinds of new opportunities and learning experiences. Over dinners, various children faithfully recite historical accounts of the holiday, describing in great detail the courage of the Maccabees in overcoming their Greek/Syrian/Seleucid oppressors, and discussing the miracle of a single flask of oil unexpectedly burning for eight days during the subsequent purification and rededication of the Temple in Jerusalem. It is this miracle of oil and light that serves as the origin of the contemporary Hanukkah celebration.

Inspired by tradition, I've purchased my first-ever menorah and diligently lit the candles from left to right (after inserting them from right to left). I've also tried my luck at dreidel (*sivivon*), a game from an era predating the Maccabees' revolt in which it was a crime for Jews to practice their religion. Back then, Jews secretly studying the Torah would hide their scriptures and pull out dreidel upon hearing footsteps of approaching soldiers.

Although practicing religion was illegal, gambling was not, and thus a little four-sided spinning top became a vehicle and eventual symbol for religion, perseverance, and miracle. (It also became the subject of a song, which explains why "My Little Dreidel" was one of the tunes performed for President Bush during last week's celebration of Hanukkah at the White House.) Although Hanukkah is variously referred to as a Celebration of "Light," "Dedication," or "Miracle of the Oil," it is also a major holiday involving food—especially food prepared in oil. I've sampled latkes, both historically authentic (fried in oil and made with cheese, fruits, or vegetables) and anachronistic (fried in oil but made with potatoes, which weren't available until centuries after the revolt). More to my liking are *sufganiyot*, holeless jelly doughnuts fried in oil and sprinkled with sugar. Finally, in an attempt to expand the tradition and yet remain consistent with the holiday's historical roots, I've vowed to drink only Maccabee beer and root for only Maccabee soccer and basketball teams during this eight-day period of celebration.

A recent Hanukkah dinner at a friend's house that included (fried) latkes, fried green beans, and fried potato wedges suddenly rekindled my surprisingly dormant addiction to American fried and related foods. A greasy spoon in the nightlife district of Jaffa is popular with the younger crowd for its (cheeseless) burgers, but they don't compare with what can be found on even a bad day in that mecca of East Lansing (Michigan) cuisine, Crunchy's. In ten weeks, I've visited American food chains only twice (a new record for me), and both times have had unexpected adventures. In my first foray into the Burger King on Dizengoff, I used the straightforward verbal approach and ordered a hamburger. The clerk was at first unsure of my request, but seemed to figure it out in time. Yet when I moved to a table and opened the sandwich, I found a mysterious white meat inside the bun. It didn't appear to be any kind of hamburger I had ever seen before, nor did my two tentative bites taste like either chicken or fish. I strongly doubted that it was literally a "ham" burger, and I dismissed any thoughts that Burger King had found its own diabolical solution to Tel Aviv's egregious problem of feline overpopulation. So its identity remained—and remains—a mystery to this day, one that I am in no hurry to solve.

I waited several weeks before trying again—this time at a Burger King in Ramat Aviv. Having learned from my previous encounter, this time I pointed to a specific picture of a burger, fries, and soft drink (the No. 4) hoping that the combination of words and visual images would elicit greater ordering success. To his credit, the clerk told me that the burger was small, and asked me if I would like to upgrade. Confident about my choice this time, however, I said that no, the No. 4 would be fine. I didn't pay much attention as the clerk went about his business until, out of the corner of my eye, I saw him folding together one of those cardboard lunchboxes that holds a kiddie meal. When he inserted a tiny burger, miniature order of fries, and Homer Simpson action figure, though, my fate became clear. Doh! The clerk made a point of watching my face as he handed me my No. 4; but determined to uphold the dignity of Americans throughout the world, I merely smiled, thanked him, and marched away from the counter with my head held high and a colorful cardboard lunchbox proudly by my side.

The Tel Aviv beach continues to mesmerize me as much today as it did upon my arrival. I try to walk to it daily. If working late, I'll go there at around 10 or 11 P.M. and walk barefoot in the sand, listening to the crash of the surf and scanning the sky for the blinking lights of a jet, making its descent over the

Mediterranean in preparation for a landing at Ben Gurion Airport. I am never concerned about personal safety during these late-night walks, as street crime is far less common here than in the States. If I am lucky and can get away from work early, I visit the beach at sunset. What appears daily on the canvas of the Mediterranean skyline is far more beautiful than any art I've ever paid to see or own. Better yet, every day offers an entirely new and unique creation, one that unfolds as performance art before my very eyes in light and dark blues, deep pinks, and luminescent golds. Calm reigns above the skyline, action below.

Today is a particularly resplendent day on the sand: sunny and, like a typical Michigan mid-December day, about twenty degrees . . . of course, twenty degrees Celsius rather than Fahrenheit, so people are walking in open sandals rather than furry boots. Near the large hotels, I pass the usual Saturday sights and sounds of dancers spinning and clapping to strains of traditional folk songs, as well as the "whap" of hard rubber balls striking wooden paddles in ubiquitous games of *matkot*. Now peacefully situated on a concrete bench, to my far left I can see the crash of waves on the rocks near the ancient walls of St. Peter's Church. Nearby, some thirty surfers in wetsuits resemble penguins as they scoot about on their boards in all directions, hoping to catch the one great wave. In front of me, gusts of wind drag a parasailer across the sand, while a small black-and-white pup hops and barks at the odd sight of a man "running" with motionless legs. On the right, a trio of Russians strain to do chin-ups at an exercise station, while two young lovers embrace in the glow of the setting sun. My peaceful assimilation of this cavalcade of images comes to a screeching halt as a loud (and rare) group of tourists pause a few feet away and start calling to me and taking photos of me lounging on my bench. Capturing images of authentic "natives" for their friends back home, they want me to smile, wave, and tip my cap to them.

Guess I must be starting to blend in.

WEEK 12: TRAVELS

WHAT TURNED OUT TO BE a whirlwind week
began last Saturday night at 10 P.M., when a reporter from the
Jerusalem Post conducted a telephone interview with me about my
work in the area of public health policy. She had heard that I
would be addressing the director-general and Ministry of Health
in January, and wanted to feature the topic of my talk in an
upcoming news story. Of equal interest to her were my impres-
sions of Israel so far, as well as my internal struggle about coming here to teach and conduct research in the first place. Why
did I still come to Israel if I knew there was violence here? Wasn't
I afraid? It seems that many American speakers and consultants
have canceled their visits to Israel in recent weeks (because of
the violence), meaning that those of us who followed through
are appreciated a little more and regarded as something of a
pleasant novelty.

The next morning, Sunday, I set off with a colleague on a
southern trek to Negev, headed for the annual meeting of
the Israel Communication Association. Unfortunately, we got

sidetracked on the way and ended up near a rather precarious area. How near? I can't say in terms of the familiar American metric of "as the crow flies." But one person with whom I spoke answered my question using an Israeli distance metric, saying that we were "within mortar distance" of Gaza. I think that's a little farther than "a stone's throw." But in any case, the gods were smiling on us this day, and we arrived at the conference without incident. I was the only presenter speaking in English at the entire conference, including my plenary session of four speakers on the topic of "Media and Terrorism." It was a little disconcerting to sit there and not understand anything my fellow panelists were saying, especially since I knew that I could soon be unknowingly duplicating or contradicting my colleagues in a few minutes when I finally got up to offer my remarks. Fortunately, however, an extraordinarily patient and helpful colleague motioned for me to leave the stage and join her in the front row of the auditorium, where she proceeded to translate my fellow panelists' presentations. As I headed back up to the podium to give my remarks, I recalled the words of two veteran Hebrew University professors at our initial Fulbright orientation session. "When you're giving a presentation to Israelis," they had said, "realize that whatever you say, they'll tell you you're wrong. But if by some miracle you convince them that you are right, then they will simply tell you that the point you've made is trivial." Although I didn't encounter this particular response following my presentation, I did get the distinct impression that my comments were regarded as too upbeat, and not sufficiently critical of the media's performance in covering the "War on Terrorism" and subsequent bioterrorism attacks in America. A heavy dose of criticism, I've learned, is expected when the topics of terrorism, government, and media coverage converge.

On Tuesday, it was back to Tel Aviv and another lecture on "Media and Terrorism"—this time to about a hundred students in an upper-level class at Tel Aviv University. Lecturing to students about terrorism here is quite different from how I would expect it to be in America (I left before having a chance to find out in the fall). After living through intifadas, multiple suicide bombings, and hundreds of shootings throughout their lifetimes, students are already intimately familiar with the topic and its implications for public opinion dynamics, and hence do not find it new or unfamiliar whatsoever. They are also surprisingly savvy about international news organizations, and have fairly sophisticated lay theories about which ones they believe to be biased in favor of Palestinians or Israelis, and why. The result is often lively discussion based on knowledge, personal experience, and well-founded opinion, as it was on this day as well.

On Wednesday, I drove with colleagues to Jerusalem to speak at a public health policy conference in the morning, and then raced via taxi through heavy rains to the Mount Scopus campus of Hebrew University to give a colloquium on "Communication Campaigns and Effects" in the afternoon. Both were lively sessions in which attendees offered the usual keen insights and provocative questions that I have come to expect from Israeli audiences.

Thursday found me back in my regular Tel Aviv classroom, lecturing about cross-cultural research on embarrassment. At several social gatherings, this topic has elicited considerable interest from my Israeli colleagues. When I ask what embarrasses Israelis, the first response is invariably "nothing," as they go on to tell me that they are a very direct and open people, and not easily embarrassed by anything. But with a little encouragement, I soon hear about all kinds of situations regarded as embarrassing. In my class, the students could completely understand why a majority of Spaniards find it embarrassing to be slapped in public. And they empathized with Koreans who are embarrassed if they enter a room in which someone is dressing. But they were absolutely baffled by why anyone would be embarrassed about being seen with laundry hanging outside to dry. After all, it's an extremely common sight in Tel Aviv. Next, we moved to a discussion of what embarrasses Israeli students in particular. Two situations quickly emerged: (1) talking about someone who they don't realize can hear or (in the case of foreigners) understand them, and (2) trying to park a car. The gender dynamics of the latter, in particular, are quite volatile, especially if a woman is doing the parking and a man is watching or—worse yet—waiting (impatiently) in a car behind. Men are not shy about offering unsolicited "advice" upon encountering a woman attempting to navigate her car into a tight space on these narrow, crowded streets, and sparks can really fly in the ensuing "conversation."

Through with my full slate of interviews and presentations for the week, on Friday I began a tour of some historical sites. One of my longtime hobbies is learning about the Crusader period, launched in 1095 when Pope Urban II inspired thousands of Christian European peasants, noblemen, clerics, and even children to forsake their homes, their families, their possessions, and their lives to trudge across unfamiliar mountains and deserts for two full years, only to endure surprise attacks, treachery, disease, and famine during several ill-fated attempts to wrest control of the Holy Lands from various Muslim caliphs and their armies. It surprises me to hear how American Christians are shocked upon learning that contemporary Muslims are willing to sacrifice their lives in exchange for spiritual salvation. A millenium ago, it was the Christian crusaders who were willing to face near-certain death for their own religious convictions. Today's trip is to Acre, north of Tel Aviv, where I find myself walking through the various quarters of this original Crusader city and actually touching the 900-year-old tombstone of the former archbishop of Nazareth. I can see remnants of the church where Christian nuns, fearing the imminent downfall of their city-fortress, hid and cut off their noses in an attempt to prevent being raped by the approaching Egyptian Mamluks (who, outraged that the women had done such a thing, "merely" killed them instead). And I can almost hear the loud voices of the exploitive Genoese and Venetian sailors, bargaining for huge tracts of land in exchange for providing much-needed supplies to their starving and besieged fellow Christians.

My busy week would come to an end the next day, Saturday, in the Arab village of Abu Ghosh. Here, in the hills overlooking Jerusalem, I can almost envision the spot where hundreds of Crusaders reportedly lay on the ground exhausted, catching some much-needed rest before resuming their grueling march to the Holy City. (To digress a bit: Upon their arrival they were filled with a combination of awe and despair at the sight of the formidable walled city of their dreams. Either in an effort to boost morale or as the result of true divine inspiration, spiritual advisors told the Crusaders that if they repented, fasted, and marched barefoot around the walled fortress nine times, the city would fall. Soon thereafter, Muslim soldiers looked on in amazement and mocked the bedraggled procession of barefoot princes, soldiers, pilgrims, and priests—diseased, fatigued, and thirsting in the hot summer sun, circling the city in hopes of fulfilling their spiritual destiny. Amazingly enough, the predictions held true, and one thousand years later, Muslims still have not forgiven the Christian world for the mind-boggling slaughter that ensued.)

But back in Abu Ghosh . . . I was amazed at how differently I felt compared to my initial visit during my first week in Israel. Back then, surrounded by bin Laden clones in the immediate aftermath of 9/11, I felt like a duck in a shooting gallery. But on this day, I felt completely at ease. The "new" church in the village, a youngster at a mere eighty years of age, is now the site of weekly concerts. Today's program featured Handel's *Messiah* in its entirety, performed by the Upper Galilee Choir and the Symphonette Ra'anana Orchestra. Though these groups would not be regarded in the same musical league as, for example, the Israel Philharmonic, on this particular day they were spectacular. The tenor's voice sounded like honey on warm toast, while the choir was loud and animated, pushed by a conductor setting a lively tempo. It was truly inspiring to be sitting there, listening to the fervor and intensity of those singers and musicians. Following enthusiastic applause, the performers repeated a rousing encore of the "Hallelujah Chorus," inviting the audience to sing along. Though I have probably sat through more than twenty performances of this work in my lifetime, none has ever left me with the feeling that I had on this resplendently sunny day in a modest church nestled in the hills overlooking Jerusalem, surrounded by hundreds of people singing the inspiring words of a beautiful musical composition for the ages.

WEEK 13: CHRISTMAS

FRIENDS HERE TELL ME that once the chill of winter hits, Israelis will talk less because they have to keep their hands in their pockets.

Maybe it hasn't gotten cold enough yet, but so far I haven't seen any evidence of diminished communication.

It's Christmas in the Holy Land, and yet everyone seems to be talking about the most recent puerile spat between Israeli Prime Minister Sharon and Palestinian Authority Chairman Yasser Arafat. Since 1995, Arafat has attended the Midnight Mass in Bethlehem, the only Muslim national leader to do so. This year, Sharon prohibited him from visiting Bethlehem, saying that Arafat should instead spend his time tracking down the killers of former Minister of Tourism Rehavam Ze'evi. Arafat originally said that if he had to, he would walk the entire sixteen miles from Ramallah to Bethlehem in defiance of Sharon's edict. But instead, he remained in his office and met with sympathetic religious leaders from around the globe.

The spin doctors have been hard at work all week. World

political and religious leaders and the international media have pretty much universally condemned Sharon's decision, rival Israeli factions have squabbled about it, and Sharon's own Foreign Ministry has given up trying to explain it. Meanwhile, Israel's media have devoted vast amounts of coverage to the alleged public relations repercussions of the event, reaching the conventional, if somewhat fatalistic, conclusion that it's a coup for the Palestinians and a disaster for Israel that undercuts recent successes in the battle for global opinion. Of course, this is too simplistic an assessment, as there is method in what appears to be political madness. At the very least, Sharon's decision sends an unambiguous message that the Palestinian universally acknowledged as the most powerful of his people is, in fact, quite powerless—a message that Sharon has tried to convey in recent weeks by dismissing Arafat as "irrelevant."

Meanwhile, over in Bet Shemesh, a Jewish elementary school teacher staged a burning of a copy of the New Testament to protect his sixth-grade students from the messages of Christianity, an act that elicited support from his rabbi, but condemnation from the Ministry of Education and citizens who remember with horror the book burnings of Nazi Germany.

And from Jerusalem, there's a report about how Muslims control the keys to the Church of the Holy Sepulcher, built on the site where Christ was crucified and buried. It seems that various Christian factions kept fighting among themselves over important issues such as who would get to sweep which part of the Church floor, and so in the interests of keeping peace, the Muslims literally were handed the keys to the kingdom.

But if I am focusing on politics rather than on the historical and spiritual aspects of the season, there is an explanation. After more than four decades of spending this time of year immersed in symbols referring to the original Christmas in this portion of the world, I find myself, ironically, in this portion of the world with nary a symbol or trace of Christmas in sight. It's just another week at the office, especially here in Tel Aviv.

I had hoped to capture some Christmas spirit by spending December 24 in the little town of Bethlehem; but in recent weeks it has become a shooting range, and now the center of this latest controversy involving Sharon and Arafat. So I decided to head to Nazareth, a more stable Arab city and another major center of Christianity in this country. Nazareth is the village in which the Archangel Gabriel is said to have announced to Mary that she would conceive the Christ child, and a locale in which Christ himself reportedly spent a number of years. Surely I would find Christmas spirit there.

As beautiful and remarkable a city as it is, Nazareth seemed a little sad this year. Hardly any tourists were visible on the streets, and shop clerks were still trying to unload merchandise from the disappointing millennium Christmas two years ago. The city is racked by its own internal politics as Muslims are trying to erect a huge mosque near the main Christian church, much to the dismay of the Christians who consider this city sacred. Shunned by Jews because of their ethnicity (Arab), and shunned by fellow Arabs because of their religion (Christian), the Arab Christians are universally acknowledged as being wedged between a rock and a hard place, and many are leaving their homes and homeland in despair, in hopes of finding a better life abroad.

Nevertheless, on this particular day, thousands of Arab Christians lined the streets for the annual Christmas parade leading to the magnificent Basilica of the Annunciation, the work of Italian architects and the largest building of its kind in the entire Middle East. The parade, which was to wind through numerous neighborhoods throughout the city, began at 3:00 in the afternoon, and was led by religious leaders of many denominations. Following in close proximity were dozens of youth groups, their members dressed in matching uniforms and waving colorful banners and flags. The boom of drums and the unmistakable drone of bagpipes filled the air: the output of dozens of marching bands accompanying the youth groups. Serving as dividers between groups were pickup trucks carrying Christmas floats and children dressed as nativity characters, waving to the spectators, some throwing candy and small trinkets.

The crowd itself was as marvelous as the parade. Hundreds of children dressed in Santa Claus outfits and masks ran around the streets, laughing and playing—a scene similar to what might be seen at Halloween in the United States. Many lit fireworks, punctuating the sounds of bagpipes and drums with staccato crackles and blasts. At 5 P.M., though, the real fireworks display began, sending beautiful rockets high into the air over the Basilica and throngs of spectators below. From the balcony of St. Gabriel's Hotel, a restored monastery nestled high in the hills overlooking the city, the twinkling lights in the valley below served as a sparkling backdrop for the dramatic bursts of red, green, and gold in the early evening sky.

The climax of the celebration was the traditional "Midnight" Mass, held at 7:30 P.M. Admission to the mass was by ticket only, and security was reasonably tight. The Basilica is an impressive structure, with two especially interesting features. First, it is home to a collection of large visual depictions of the Annunciation, each donated by a different country and cast in various media, including wood and ceramic tile. These images range from fairly traditional (France) to somewhat gaudy high-tech (Guess who?) in appearance, but all are quite beautiful. The second striking feature is the large, dark, gaping hole in the middle of the church floor. Down below is a grotto that reveals some of the ancient stones and columns on which earlier churches were built centuries before. But during the mass, this hole seems to symbolize the darkness of the lonely netherworld that sits below, in stark contrast to the warm and comforting lights, music, and community in the ethereal world above. It makes for quite a dramatic and compelling effect.

Although this is one of the pre-eminent Christian sites in the Holy Land, the Basilica was nowhere near full on this most important night of the year. When about a hundred Nigerian tourists, all sporting baseball-style caps with tour company logos, departed in unison midway through the service, only the locals and a small smattering of other tourists remained. The service itself was imposing, displaying the full weight and imperial majesty of the Roman Church. One bishop and eleven priests said parts of the mass in at least six languages: Latin, Italian, French, English, Arabic, and Hebrew. With liberal applications of incense and elaborate ritual no longer seen in American services, it was a powerful, if somewhat impersonal, spectacle. Yet with the familiar strains of the "Hallelujah Chorus" emanating from the massive choir at the end of the service, I finally started to feel filled with the Christmas spirit that had heretofore eluded me this season.

Shalom and Happy New Year from afar.

The majestic main entrance to Tel Aviv University. Inscribed on paved squares under-foot are tributes to intellectual giants of the ages.

Creative parking on Shlomo Hamelekh (King Solomon), my neighborhood in Tel Aviv.

The "deserted" winter beach of Tel Aviv.

In front of the Dolphinarium on the Tel Aviv beach, a memorial to youths killed in a suicide bomb attack.

Behind the dolphinarium on the Tel Aviv beach, drummers congregate to welcome the Friday sunset.

Caesarea: home to Romans, Crusaders, Jews, Samaritans, Byzantines, Mamluks, Muslims, and other peoples over the millenia.

Inside the excavated refectory of St. John's, in the former Crusader fortress (and current Arab city) of Acre (Acco).

Bagpipers in the annual Christmas parade, the Arab city of Nazareth.

The dry moat of the Crusader castle Belvoir, overlooking the resplendent Jordan Valley, Sea of Galilee and the snow-capped peaks of Syria's Mount Hermon.

Security guards and shoppers near Dizengoff Center, Tel Aviv.

Sandbags at an outdoor café, Tel Aviv.

Media camera crew at the site of a suicide bombing in Jerusalem. In the background is a refrigerator which will store recovered body fragments until burial.

Members of ZAKA, a rapid response team of volunteer ultra-orthodox, search for remains in the aftermath of the bombing.

Friday afternoon at the Arts and Crafts Market on Nachlat Binyamin, Tel Aviv.

The Yitzak Rabin Memorial on Ibn Gvirol, Tel Aviv.

WEEK 14: VIGNETTES

THE RUST-COLORED CAT stops and stares, eyes fixated on the alluring prize that looms within striking distance. It wiggles back and forth, crouching lower and lower, twirling its tail rhythmically in the air, waiting for just the right moment to spring into action. Suddenly and ruthlessly it attacks, snatching and clutching its prey. It curls into a ball while its clawed feet furiously shred and tear this diabolical creature disguised as a scrunched-up wad of paper. Nearby, a cigarette smoker, blissfully ignoring the "No Smoking" ordinance in the building, casts a passing glance at the carnage below. And a patient, hooked up to and pushing his own IV stand, gives both a wide berth as he slowly saunters down the corridor of this large suburban hospital.

· · ·

Tonight's goal: finding a parking place in downtown Tel Aviv—a task only slightly less daunting than locating Osama bin

Laden. Suddenly, a man in his sixties, wearing sandals, bursts out into the middle of the street, blocks traffic, waves, and points to his car. *Finally! Success!* One catch, though: he seems to need assistance. The man motions for us to pull close to his engine so he can use our car's battery to start his. He seems oblivious to the idea that the five or six drivers waiting in line behind would object; surely they have nothing to better to do at 10 P.M. on a Thursday night.

The din of horns and angry shouts fills the air from behind as the man stands and deliberates about how to attach the cables, shuffles ever so slowly over to the passenger's side of his car, slides across to the driver's side to start it, slides back to the passenger's side to exit, shuffles back over to unhook the cables, and then sends a shower of sparks into the air when he carelessly tugs the cables off our battery. The drivers behind us have graduated from furious to homicidal by now, their own car batteries drained from relentless honking over the twenty or so minutes that they have been stuck here. Finally, the man is all set and climbs back into his car. But wait . . . Why is he waving us on? Seems he is not moving after all, but just wanted a jumpstart so that he could rev his engine without giving up his precious parking space.

· · ·

The tall, lanky woman with the high cheekbones and designer-blond hair is leaning against a road sign on a dark and desolate stretch of road near Tel Baruch Beach, the heart of the outdoor commercial sex district. Upon catching a glimpse of our car's headlights, she starts strutting toward us, exhibiting the moves of a runway model. Farther up, two other ghostly apparitions beckon with a provocative wave from the other side of this unlit and otherwise deserted road. Then another, and another . . . The women—er, people—are clothed in designer garments more exotic than can be seen in the Okemos (Michigan) Big Boy Restaurant on prom night, sequins glittering in reflected light like the twinkling stars above. Rumors abound about the identities of their clients, who allegedly arrive in buses to meet them out here in this desolate spot. But rumor is rumor, and discretion must remain the word for this evening.

• • •

Walking on a busy, Friday afternoon along a bustling, crowded Sheinkin Street—home to numerous designer boutiques and chic cafés. Suddenly I hear an accordion playing the familiar strains of "On the Street Where You Live" from the musical My Fair Lady. The sounds are coming from a little man, probably in his seventies, sitting in a small, dented folding chair on the sidewalk up ahead. His weathered cheeks sag inward where teeth once stood. On his head is a blue Edwardian crushed-velvet hat with protruding red and yellow roses, one pointed left, the other headed right. He is wearing a bright red, mid-thigh-length jacket, with multicolored scarves flowing from his wrists, and matching bright red pants. On his feet are sandals connected to what appear to be small cafeteria trays, to which tambourines are also attached. Without missing a beat, he shakes his foot and dips his head in appreciation as a music-loving passerby donates a spare shekel.

• • •

The blare of a loud and unpleasant alarm jars my daydreams while I'm standing in the supermarket checkout line. A man carrying a motorcycle helmet has mistakenly entered the "emergency exit" door and set off a ruckus. Dozens of people are gazing at him with their sternest death stares etched in their faces. The supermarket manager storms over to him and chastises him for his dramatic and unpleasant entrance. What will the bumbling motorcyclist do now? Probably turn red, look contrite, and mumble an apology to the newly deafened customers and staff . . . right? Not quite. Indignant that the manager would dare to scold him, he launches into a tirade and yells right back, the two of them carrying on in animated fashion, yelling and gesturing vigorously while the alarm continues to blare, and I take my bag and head for the relative peace and quiet of the busy streets outside.

. . .

5—4—3—2—1!

Happy Sylvester!

A moment after the stroke of midnight, it is now year 2002, and about a hundred people in this packed café on Rothschild have stopped waving their sparklers and are now leaning over their café tables to kiss their beloved. A woman at an adjacent table gets up, walks around, and sits on her boyfriend's lap to give him a more inspired token of her affection. Though Israelis celebrated the Jewish New Year earlier in the Fall, many are out partying again tonight, and cafés, bars, and restaurants are decorated and packed. December 31 is called "Sylvester," though many people here don't exactly know why. In fact, Sylvester was a Catholic saint and pope who died and was buried on December 31 in the year 335. Unknown even to most American Christians, his name, at least, is honored annually in parties and cafés here in the homeland of Judaism, as a result of immigration that has introduced new customs, as well as new people, to this land.

. . .

On Nachlat Binyamin, near Hacarmel Market now—at the outdoor street fair, where artists of all types congregate to promote and sell their wares. The woman tending my favorite booth is very friendly, as she should be with someone who has purchased enough of her wares to subsidize a modest addition to her house. Soon, we're chatting up a storm, and now that I've purchased my fourth item and am admiring a fifth, she asks if I have family here. "No," I say, adding that I am just here on my own. With that, she unexpectedly offers me an attractive price on the fifth item that I have been considering. And casually adds that her daughter, who is studying cosmetology, will be joining her in the booth in fifteen minutes.

WEEK 15: WOMEN

ON THE SURFACE, Israel would seem to be a pretty hospitable environment for women these days. After all, it is a country in which, early in its history, a woman was elected prime minister, and a country in which women's representation in the Knesset is currently at an all-time high. Women serve as generals, members of the Supreme Court, mayors of cities, directors of institutes, and leaders of corporations. But, as is the case for most things over here, reality is a little more complicated than appearances, and Israel, like many Middle Eastern societies, can be quite a challenging environment in which to be a woman.

Some feminist critics argue that it all starts with traditional Jewish law (*halakhah*), which they claim is rooted in Orthodox religious tradition that fundamentally favors the rights of men and treats women as property. The *halakhah*, for example, privileges men at the expense of women in conflicts involving family law, especially in cases of divorce. Reflecting the complexity of the law, five different friends have so far explained divorce laws to me in five different—and contradictory—ways; but at least all agree that men have the upper hand. But the law can disadvantage women in peaceful marriages as well: if a husband is presumed dead or disappears without first giving his wife a "get" or release, his widow may experience considerable hardship in her future. The significance of this type of case was recently illustrated in a poignant story about September 11. A Jewish man in one of the Twin Towers reportedly gave his wife a "get" in a recorded telephone conversation as the building was collapsing around him. Without record of his approval and conclusive proof of his death, his widow would have faced the prospect of life as an *agunah*: single, with no prospect of remarriage and uncertain financial support.

The Israeli military has long been the target of sustained feminist criticism for its virtually impenetrable glass ceilings that, until recently, have denied women opportunities for advancement to the top echelons of command. Some opportunities are limited by regulations that keep women soldiers out of combat, and thus out of situations in which they can sow the seeds for promotion through acts of heroism or ingenuity (though, as a male friend noted, they are more likely to stay alive, too). Other opportunities are limited by sensitivities to cultural norms about the role of women in neighboring Arab countries, particularly in units that must work closely with counterparts in Egypt or Jordan. Since military careers build social networks and are vital stepping-stones for careers in corporate management and government office, the military culture has long been blamed for limiting women's opportunities for leadership positions upon discharge.

But it would be unfair to single out the military. Rarely, if ever, have I attended a reception in my own industry—higher education—without hearing at least one horror story of a woman faculty member unfairly denied promotion, or passed over for deserved opportunities and rewards. A number of women whom I encounter are downright demoralized because of what they see as structural discrimination, deeply embedded in the university system. In one particularly galling case for women here, a professor who drafted the language for the national law on sexual harassment was denied tenure at Hebrew University. And a secular woman unanimously chosen by her colleagues to serve as chairperson of the music department at Bar-Ilan University, an institution with deep religious roots, had her appointment rescinded by upper administration—a decision that one (male) colleague labeled "an unparalleled scandal." More generally, only about 8 percent of all (senior) professors in Israel are women, compared to 40 percent of all (junior) lecturers. In the words of one angry local columnist, "One possible explanation is that women have no brains. Only men are born with the gene for academic brilliance. This is the accepted explanation in Afghanistan."

Problems encountered by women in the workplace are by no means restricted to the realms of the military and higher education. Some twenty thousand Filipino au pairs and housekeepers, brought to the country illegally without permits, often work in arduous conditions and under the constant fear of expulsion. A recent news story reported how one such woman was forced to work sixteen-hour workdays and be responsible for cooking, laundry, ironing, childcare, elder care, and physical therapy. Not allowed to take warm showers, the woman said she was paid less than she had been promised, and felt treated like a servant. Because these women are especially vulnerable, their employers have been known to abuse them, and keep them around by threatening to accuse them of theft, threatening to have them deported if they try to leave.

Another recent news report described the plight of women from Eastern Europe, smuggled into Israel with promises of "great" working conditions, but instead raped and sold into prostitution. Some 90 percent of Israeli prostitutes are reportedly Russian women who have been smuggled in through Egypt by organized crime. Once in Israel, they are reportedly allowed to keep a mere 10 shekels (about $2.50) of the 200 they earn for servicing each client. Still worse, if intercepted while being smuggled across the border, they often have been merely returned to Egypt, rather than liberated and allowed to return to their homes.

Other recent exposés have shocked the country with reports of women who, as young girls, were sexually abused in kibbutzim. Now adults, several of these women are suffering long-term psychological consequences of their experiences, mired in feelings of betrayal and abandonment because of parents and administrators who reportedly failed to report the abuse to police for years.

For Arab women, life can be difficult in very different ways. For starters, their opportunities for education and careers are severely limited, and they earn only about 70 percent of what Jewish women make—which, of course, is only a percentage of what Jewish men make. But far more dangerous, the policy of femicide, or "honor killing," is still recognized as "legitimate" (though unlawful) punishment for a woman who commits adultery or otherwise dishonors her family in some Arab communities within Israel. In one recent case, family members apparently stoned a woman to death after following her to her illicit rendezvous with her lover.

In sharing a draft of the above with women friends here, I received two reactions that really surprised me. First, I learned that while many women are openly critical of discrimination and harassment in their workplace, most don't tend to consider the experiences of Filipino housekeepers, Russian prostitutes, and Arab women as relevant to their own situation. Ethnicity seems to be a far more important bond than gender, and hence the experiences of non-Jewish women are viewed not so much as gender discrimination as part of an unrelated struggle.

Second, although the women agreed with the facts of what I had written, they asked me to include a caveat so that Israel wouldn't be portrayed so negatively to the rest of the world (a concern about image shared, incidentally, by men and women, young and old). Admittedly, in some ways what I've written in this letter may be a classic illustration of how the sum of the parts can appear greater (or in this case, worse) than the whole. True, the "macho" culture of the military and the patriarchal foundations of the law may disadvantage women, but the culture also offers numerous opportunities for women that are not found elsewhere in the Middle East. Sexual abuse, low wages, and glass ceilings are all familiar topics throughout the Americas and Europe, and it would be unfair to suggest that these phenomena are much more pronounced here than elsewhere.

Nevertheless, in my conversations with a broad cross-section of people, I get the distinct impression that a growing segment of secular and non-Jewish Tel Aviv women, in particular, are resentful of public policies, often rooted in ancient Jewish tradition, which they see as limiting their freedoms, denying their voices, and even threatening their lives. Until now, they haven't had the political power, institutional structures, or organized presence to elicit the reforms that they have sought. But at least they see some reason for hope. For the first time in

Israel's history, the government has established a ministerial committee to promote women's rights. Ever conscious of appearances, and comfortable with military metaphors, Prime Minister Sharon has even hailed this landmark development as "an important battle for the image of Israeli society."

WEEK 16: NUMBERS

SITTING HERE SHIVERING in my apartment as I type, it's hard to imagine that only eight days ago I was walking along the beach in a T-shirt and jeans. But a solid week of cold winds, fantastic thunderstorms, and soft, delicate drizzles has given me newfound appreciation for the legend of Noah's Ark, as well as for a Michigan fireplace. The rain is welcomed and needed because aquifers and surface bodies of water are perilously depleted. And although Michigan residents stuck in snowdrifts may not be especially sympathetic to complaints about lightly falling snow and near-zero temperatures in nearby Jerusalem, the nature of cold weather is quite different here than in the upper Midwest. Buildings and apartments are built for a desert-like climate, and many have no insulation or built-in sources of heat. The windows in my apartment, which never completely close, seem designed to provide year-round ventilation, a problem in January. The tile floors, installed to provide coolness underfoot, are appreciated in summer but cursed in winter. Tap water is cold, warmed only after a flick of a switch on a manual water heater, followed by a long wait. Even furniture is cold, as it sits in unheated rooms and corridors day and night. And so, for most of the week, I have been wearing a Polartec jacket and shoes around my apartment, peering at the storms through the small area of a window visible around the towel plugging the many holes and gaps in the frame, and sitting inches away from a portable heater.

The foul weather has afforded an unexpected opportunity to catch up on my reading and current events, some of which I am passing along in the form of brief adaptations of news notes and stories published over the past few months in the English-language version of *Ha'aretz*. These figures, which I'm not in a position to verify independently of their appearance in the newspaper, provide some numerical snapshots of Israel that may or may not have been reported widely in the U.S. press.

1   The number of extra flights that an ultra-Orthodox rabbi took to fly from Tel Aviv to London in order to bypass an international flight path that passes over a cemetery. He originally planned to take a direct flight and wrap himself in an opaque paper bag when the plane would fly over the cemetery, but airline security regulations would not permit him to do so. So he rented a private plane to fly to Cyprus, where he then picked up a flight to London.

4   The number of lines that a group of Palestinians reportedly were told to form by soldiers at a West Bank checkpoint: one for "old men," one for "young men," one for "pretty women," and one for "ugly women." When the women weren't sure where to stand, the Israeli soldiers began assigning them.

12   The percentage of Israeli women academics working in the

natural sciences, according to a new survey in twelve European nations by the "Helsinki Group on Women." The average across Europe is 26%.

18   The percentage of audience segments defined as "sports fans" and "anti-Israelis" in a recent profile of Israeli television viewers commissioned by Channel Three. An additional 12% were labeled "self-proclaimed intellectuals," 12% "soap opera enthusiasts," 11% "Seinfelders," 11% "middle-of-the-roaders," 9% "news lovers," and 9% "young viewers."

21   The approximate percentage of draft-age male youths who were not drafted in 2000, up from 19.8% in 1999. The figures showed that nearly half cited religious reasons for not enlisting, while the rest were rejected for medical reasons, being abroad, or unfit for other reasons, such as criminal record. Among women, 27.5% did not serve, mostly for religious reasons.

40   The percentage of income earners who do not earn enough to pay taxes, and hence pay no tax. Israel's highest and lowest income segments reportedly assume the lowest tax burden in the Western world, while the middle-income earners assume the highest.

55   The percentage increase, over the past five years, in the number of students at yeshivas, with a corresponding cost of tens of thousands of shekels to taxpayers. According to a *Ha'aretz* editorial, figures on yeshiva enrollments include thousands of fictitious students who, if revealed, would substantially reduce or eliminate the need for any additional subsidies to the yeshivas.

63   The percentage of Israelis who report an "overall positive opinion" of Britain, according to a survey of Israeli perceptions commissioned by the British Embassy. While respondents consider Britain to be Israel's second-best friend after

the United States, only 26% said they believe that Britain supports Israel in the Arab-Israeli conflict.

230   The amount, in shekels, of a proposed fine as part of legislation that would ban the use of cell phones in restaurants, cafés, buses, hospitals, airports, and government offices. The two sponsors of the legislation claim that the constant ringing of phones has made public places "unbearable."

1,773   The number of police requests for permission to wiretap suspects' phones approved by the courts last year. In comparison, four requests were denied.

3,200   The amount, in shekels, that Hebrew University is charging students to cover security expenses associated with the visit to the campus of Foreign Minister Shimon Peres, who is delivering a talk to the New Horizon student group. The group's political coordinator says that the demand for payment will effectively put an end to future visits to the campus by Peres.

11,631   The number of Jewish students who attend pre-university preparatory institutes. In comparison, 369 Arab students attend these institutes.

16,000   The number of cats that have been spayed or neutered in the seven years since Tel Aviv instituted its program to reduce the feline population in the city. An estimated 5,000 families feed cats in Tel Aviv, some providing sustenance to as many as 50 or 60. The total number of cats in Tel Aviv is unknown, though it is estimated in the tens of thousands.

26,800   The number of non-Jews who immigrated to Israel in 2000. In comparison, there were 26,200 Jews who immigrated to Israel in the same period.

38,500   The number of Israelis expected to pay an average of $1,000 to go abroad and ski this year, an increase of about 10% over last year. Around 90% of the skiers are headed to France,

Italy, and Austria, with Andorra becoming an increasingly popular destination.

234,000 The number of unemployed Israelis in the third quarter of 2001, a record high in the history of the country.

525,000 The estimated number of Israeli children living below the poverty line in 2001. Of developed nations, Israel ranks second (to Mexico) in the incidence of child poverty.

7 billion The estimated cost of road accidents to the Israeli economy in 2000, a figure that includes loss of productivity, property damage, hospitalization, etc.

13 billion The estimated direct cost so far, in shekels, of the intifada, a figure that doesn't include indirect costs from lower consumer spending, drop in investments, or loss of income.

WEEK 17: POLITICS

SURVEY RESEARCH APPEARS to be an especially challenging undertaking in Israel. With the threat of violence always in the air, Arabs tend to be suspicious of strangers calling to ask for their political attitudes, and often decline to participate. The attitudes of Russian immigrants are often underrepresented as well, because of language barriers. Compulsory military service sends a high proportion of young adults out of households and onto military bases, excluding them from samples. Many Christian Nigerian and Filipino workers are in the country without permits, and are regularly excluded from samples as well. And the most religious Jews rarely participate in surveys at all, but when they do, are known to give misleading responses. Researchers attempt to compensate for these conundrums through statistical weighting, which may not really solve these problems, even as it introduces new ones. Nevertheless, I'm confident that some population groups actually do participate in surveys here, and that survey research does a fine job of representing their views.

Earlier this week I had the opportunity to dine with several survey researchers from assorted institutes around the country. Accompanying after-dinner coffee and tea was a new story relating survey research and the ultra-Orthodox. It seems that a local polling firm once made the mistake of trying to complete interviews every night of the week, including Friday and Saturday. Some of the weekend telephone calls, as can happen with random-digit dialing, reached homes of the ultra-Orthodox. Although most of these people usually refuse to answer their phones on the Sabbath altogether, some apparently did—perhaps thinking that the call was a life-and-death emergency—and learned the identity of the telephone intruders.

The next day a group of them got together and apparently tried to burn down the building in which the polling firm was based.

People at the dinner party chuckled and nodded their heads in understanding. But still awaiting an ending to the story, I naively asked if the people who tried to burn the building had been arrested. "No," someone said, "of course not. It's dangerous to arrest those people." Again, people nodded in agreement, familiar with anecdotes about political figures who had challenged the ultra-Orthodox and ended up regretting it. As the conversation started to drift in a new direction, I remained stuck behind, wondering about the reaction if the fire had instead been started by either an equally devout group of religious Muslims or simply by some demented, pyromaniac Arab. Probably less chuckling, and definitely more outrage. There was, however, one question that no one could answer satisfactorily: how did the pollsters code "building burning" as an expression of public opinion? After all, it wouldn't have fit the usual closed-ended response categories. But it doesn't exactly qualify as a "non response," either.

My political acculturation continued as I read some work by a colleague on an important concept that permeates public discourse.* In the words of two scholars who also work in this area, "no description of Israeli culture would be complete without reference to the term '*freier*.'"†

What is a "*freier*"? Basically, it is a Yiddish term for "sucker" or "patsy," but with a special connotation. Whereas in America the term "sucker" refers to someone who is easily fooled or duped, in Israel the term *freier* refers to someone who plays by the rules, and in so doing, is taken advantage of and regarded as a dupe.

In interviews with American immigrants in Israel, researchers have identified specific behaviors that can earn a person the label of a *freier*: paying one's taxes in full, not cheating on an exam, standing in line without pushing ahead, abiding by hospital visiting hours, apologizing upon accidentally bumping another person on the street, opening doors for others, or stopping a car to let people cross the street.‡

Being called a *freier* is hardly a compliment; in fact, it's a real insult, a label that Israelis try to avoid. Nevertheless, a number of American immigrants apparently have maintained the behaviors of *freiers*, perhaps out of commitment to their former American ways, or in a personal campaign to instill order and civility that they believe to be lacking in Israeli society, or as a means of distancing themselves from their new culture.

* L. Bloch, "Communicating as an American Immigrant in Israel: The *Freier* Phenomenon and the Pursuit of an Alternative Value System," *Research on Language and Social Interaction*, 31, no. 2 (1998): 177–208.

† L. Shahar and D. Kurz, *Border Crossings: American Interactions with Israelis* (Yarmouth, Maine: Intercultural Press, 1995), 108.

‡ Bloch, *op cit*.

At the root of an Israeli's concern with being labeled a *freier* is a lack of trust, a condition that would appear to be problematic on numerous levels. How can politicians make the first move toward peace with their enemies when they risk being derided as *freiers* at the first sign that a truce has been broken? How can government expect its citizens to make sacrifices for the common good when doing so is regarded as the mark of a dupe? And how can people trust their fellow citizens if they believe that everyone else around them is ignoring the rules?

.　.　.

Generating many questions but few answers, my week of pondering things political was further enlivened by the arrival of former President Clinton. His visit to Israel is part of a global tour that has included lecturing in Europe, being the guest of honor at a fundraiser in Cairo a few nights ago, and now receiving an honorary doctorate here at Tel Aviv University. According to some (non-Israeli) press accounts, Clinton was concerned that the events of September 11 and the subsequent war on terrorism would deflect attention from his former presidency and potentially tarnish his legacy. So, as has happened many times in the past, he once again rallied his top advisors to strategize about how to recapture his stature in the public eye, and has been globe-trotting ever since.

If Clinton is the equivalent of a rock star in the United States, he is that and more over here. Naturally, he is deeply appreciated for his administration's substantial financial and political support of this country; but he has made an equally telling impression on a personal level as well. My octogenarian landlady gushes when relating the story of how she received a letter of congratulations from him after a local news story reported that she had received an award. And one of my students positively glows when talking about how she would eagerly jump at the chance of being his intern—anytime, anywhere.

Last night, Clinton first met with university leaders at a pre-dinner reception that was under such tight security that guests weren't told where it was until they arrived at the hotel and passed through security. With eight hundred supporters paying $1,000 per plate for the main ceremony, it was an exclusive and formal affair, totally different from the raucous, populist, and highly choreographed tribute on the MSU campus last year. Clinton, looking distinguished in his academic gown adorned with the red and black colors of Tel Aviv University, was honored for his attempts to negotiate peace in the Middle East. In an emotional and well-received speech, he encouraged Israelis to be ready for a miracle, and not to give up or give in.

By the way, the ceremony also marked the inauguration of the new Saban Center for American Studies. (And before anyone asks . . . No, there is no truth to the rumor that Nick Saban has left his contract at LSU to switch to Tel Aviv U.)*

*Soon after Michigan State University football coach Nick Saban accepted an offer of more than six million dollars to move to Louisiana State University earlier in the year, disgruntled Spartan fans made him the butt of frequent jokes, linking his name to every job vacancy announced in the local press.

WEEK 18: STEREOTYPES

ONLY THREE WEEKS LEFT!

Feels like I just got here, and now I have to start packing. Maybe it's a good time to finally check out the forty-four-page manual for overseas visitors provided by the Fulbright office (which, by the way, has been first rate—from the moment that I first sought information on this fellowship, a couple of years ago, through my exit interview earlier this week. Very organized, efficient, and personable.)

Part 5 of the manual talks about "culture shock" and warns that after the phase one "honeymoon," we may stumble into a phase two "What-am-I-doing-here?" stage, characterized by hostility, anger, and losing one's sense of humor. What might bring this about? According to the manual, ". . . problems with the phones, no fresh fruit available, cobras on the porch, you're suffering from diarrhea, you've been robbed, your job is not quite what you expected, you can't get the hang of the language . . . and to top it off the local people seem indifferent to your problems."

Let's take these one at a time.

"Problems with the phone?" Not really, other than having run up a bill of around 2,000 shekels in my first two months. That and, of course, hearing those ubiquitous cell phones ring, buzz, beep, and burp in the middle of movies, plays, and concerts. "No fresh fruit?" With the Garden of Eden allegedly having been somewhere in this general vicinity, fruit—and especially fruit juice—is ubiquitous, including exotic varieties never before seen in Lansing. "Cobras on the porch?" No, I'm still here. "Diarrhea?" No comment. "Been robbed?" Only when I buy groceries. "Unpleasant job?" With great colleagues and engaging students, my job was quite pleasant, tarnished only slightly by the month-long faculty strike that threw the semester into temporary disarray and inconvenienced students. "Can't get the hang of the language?" Not a problem, because English is virtually a co-native language. (I did learn one important local language tip, though: when pronouncing "*oy vey*," one needs to drop the shoulders, tilt the head, and simultaneously exhale on the "*oy*.") "Indifferent people?" Surrounded by doting friends, seemingly concerned with nothing other than my welfare and mental health, I have not known indifference in any way, shape, or form. As for losing my sense of humor, it happened only briefly during a three-week stretch of rain and chilly temperatures that coincided with my catching a cold and gaining two kilograms. But when winter abruptly ended, the sun reappeared, and I started paying attention again to what the politicians are saying on TV here, my sense of humor became fully reinvigorated.

The most interesting part of the Fulbright manual is the section comparing what Israelis think about Americans, what Americans think about Israelis, and what each group thinks about itself. For example, the manual says that Americans see themselves as "organized," which Israelis see instead as "rigid, 'square,' inflexible, efficient at the expense of relationships, going by the book instead of improvising." I suppose there is some truth to this. Israelis definitely value relationships and have more of a casual, Mediterranean approach to life. Rules and deadlines, to which Americans slavishly adhere, Israeli clerks seem to consider merely advisory. (One friend joked that the term "living line" is more accurate than "deadline" in describing the Israeli orientation to due dates: fluid and changeable rather than irreversible). Maybe this has something to do with traditional Jewish law having 613 commandments instead of just the ten with which most Americans are familiar; with so many rules, one has to be a little flexible. Long-range planning is almost non-existent, reflecting the unpredictability with which the future is viewed. Time is fluid, and people expect last-minute changes in plans. Reflecting their stereotypes of others' rigidity relative to their own flexibility, Israelis tell a story about three people invited to a dinner party: The first, an American, arrives a few minutes early; the second, a German, arrives precisely on time; and the third, an Israeli, will be about a half-hour late . . . that is, if his plans don't change entirely.

And what about reverse perceptions? According to the manual, whereas Israelis see themselves as "willing to take risks," Americans see people who are "irresponsible, overconfident." Absolutely right, and I see this every day in traffic. Like blood-starved mosquitoes at a picnic, scooter drivers buzz in, out, around, and behind cars and pedestrians without warning. Automobile drivers seem to treat the morning and afternoon commutes as cathartic therapy for homicidal fantasies. Turn signals are modes of communication used by only a few *freiers*. And while police are always on the lookout for violence, they don't think to look for it in the downtown traffic of Tel Aviv.

One of the best therapies for post-traumatic driving syndrome, as is the case everywhere else in the world, is returning to nature. In previous letters, I've described my profound affection for the Mediterranean and its white, sandy beaches. But when traveling outside the city, the Judean hills are a worthy alternative.

Since the country's earliest days, Israelis have been planting trees. Pines, not indigenous to the region, were planted for years because they grow fast, and politicians wanted quick results. But many pines have not fared well due to fire and disease, and so amidst the verdant shades of cypress, carob, and Mediterranean oak, there are ghostly patches of graying forest on either side of the winding road to the Mountain of the Holy People. Although it is still only January, tiny white irises, vibrant red *calaniyot*, and resilient pink *rakafot* are already starting to dot the hillsides as in an Impressionist painting. Rock wall terraces snake their way up the mountainside, while small, broken pieces of pottery crackle underfoot, the sole reminders that an Arab village once stood here.

After passing a couple of picnic areas stirring with afternoon barbecuers, we parked and started walking down a dirt road, passing numerous small, rough stone monuments along the way. The monuments are remembrances of loved ones who have passed on, forming a true memory lane in an otherwise deserted stretch of dirt, rock, and trees. Above, the silence was broken only by the distinctive whistle of a breeze rustling through the pines, a comforting sound that I remember so fondly from my days of hiking in the southern Appalachians. Below, a panoramic valley beckoned in this most serene of spots, remarkable in its sense of isolation, mere kilometers from the horrors of untold violence on one side and the relentless bustle of city traffic on the other.

Just as I was preparing to conclude and send my weekly letter, a suicide bomber struck in the heart of Tel Aviv this morning, wounding more than twenty and bringing the horror of terrorism much closer to home. The bombing happened a few days after Israeli military forces attacked and killed several Palestinians suspected of being terrorists—killings that outraged Palestinians, who promised revenge, and angered some Israelis as well. Anticipating trouble, the Tel Aviv police have been on special alert all week, and it showed today. While taking my usual Friday afternoon walk on Sheinkin, I encountered a bomb scare on a side street a couple of blocks from the McDonald's. An unidentified green knapsack had been found on the roof luggage rack of a car, and a single police officer, covered in protective garb, was investigating. In spite of the bomb attack earlier in the day, passersby seemed amazingly relaxed and unconcerned. Many were standing and watching, talking on cell phones, joking, laughing, with some even trying to walk down the side street that had been blocked off—only to be turned back by the frustrated police officer, who was unsuccessfully attempting to convey the gravity of the situation. (The atmosphere was totally different from the tense and somber mood I encountered at a similar bomb scare in Jerusalem a few weeks ago; could it be because terrorism seems so much more remote and unlikely here than there?) The policeman carefully approached the car with the suspicious package, attached two ropes, moved to a faraway spot, and tugged until the package tumbled off the car roof. It landed harmlessly on the ground with a thud, exposing several rolls of toilet paper. At about the same time, near Dizengoff Center, a second bomb scare emptied a café of its usual Friday afternoon crowd. Two false alarms a few blocks apart within minutes of each other; I'm getting the distinct impression that police believe that this morning's attack was merely a foreshadowing of things to come.

WEEK 19: PEACE

THE RUDE EARLY-MORNING *beeping* of my alarm clock interrupted my peaceful slumber and demanded a difficult decision that I had successfully delayed for seven hours: Would I struggle out of bed now and spend one of my precious last Saturdays in Israel driving in a cramped caravan through military checkpoints to volatile Ramallah to meet with Palestinian peace activists, or enjoy a relaxed morning on the Tel Aviv beach and relish the warm sunshine of early February?

Believe it or not, it wasn't an easy decision. Since arriving in Tel Aviv, I had wanted to learn more about efforts to achieve peace on both sides of the border, and here was my chance. But, in spite of feeling terrible pangs of guilt and total irresponsibility, I chose the option of a relaxing morning—another victim of a virulent strain of Tel Aviv hedonism. In many ways, my reaction (which I am not trying to excuse) was probably fairly typical of how many Tel Aviv residents react to these types of peace-seeking events: yes, they are probably important, but . . .

In the end, three hundred Israelis from around the country

proved to be more dedicated than I. They met at a central staging location, drove into the territories to Ramallah, and spent the day in discussions with Palestinian counterparts, even hearing from Yasser Arafat. Yet, although the potentially historic event was mentioned briefly on an inside page in *Ha'aretz*, it certainly didn't receive anywhere near the attention that is regularly given to even a minor act of inflammatory rhetoric or violence.

In general, judging by what is in the press, one could easily get the impression that Israelis and Palestinians are completely polarized, unwilling to even try to negotiate a peaceful solution to the current conflict. And yet, I know from personal experience that this isn't true. One time, a Palestinian cab driver in Jerusalem—whose son attends a mixed Jewish-Arab elementary school—described his comprehensive plan for peace while driving me to my destination, ending with a claim that the parents at his son's school could solve the crisis "in a day." An overly simplistic and audacious claim to be sure; nevertheless, his desire and willingness to seek a palatable middle ground and put an end to the conflict was obvious. At other times, I have personally attended Israeli peace rallies at which attendees have expressed sincere desires for peace—and willingness to make the tough compromises necessary to achieve it—only to open the paper the next day to find little or no mention of the event. To a large degree, the press seems to regard the Israeli peace movement as something that either doesn't exist or isn't viable, but in any case isn't worth writing about. Which raises the age-old question: If a peace rally falls in the middle of a forest and no one is around to hear it, does it still make a sound? In Israel these days, it rarely does, even if it falls in the middle of a public square.

Last week, a friend forwarded an e-mail to me, describing an apparently extraordinary recent rally in Jerusalem, organized by "Women for a Just Peace." I say "apparently extraordinary" because even though it attracted 5,000 Israeli and Palestinian participants; delegations from Belgium, Canada, England, France, Italy, Portugal, Spain, and the United States; and participants in 118 other locations around the world, I neither saw anything about it on television nor read anything about it in the (English-language) paper. It's pretty astonishing to me that an event of this magnitude would be ignored by the press, but it's no surprise to peace activists, who charge that the press is confusing patriotism with blind support for government policy (a phenomenon not exactly foreign to American media since September 11).

Here, according to the e-mail account, is what happened: Led by a banner reading "The Occupation Is Killing Us All," and signs depicting the states of Palestine and Israel side by side, the rally began with a "March of Mourning" that eventually led to the Old City. There, Israeli and Palestinian political and social leaders gave speeches, lit candles, listened to a concert, and acknowledged the presence of several members of the Knesset.

Altogether, some thirteen Israeli peace organizations participated, including: Bat Shalom (Israeli-Palestinian partnership of women), Gush Shalom (working to end the occupation), High School Seniors (refusing military service in occupied territories), Israeli Committee Against Home Demolitions (monitoring the demolition of Palestinian homes by Israeli military), Machsom Watch (women monitoring military checkpoints), Mothers and Women for Peace (formerly the 4 Mothers Movement that was influential in ending Israeli occupation in Lebanon), New Profile (supporting conscientious objectors), Peace Now (calling for an end to settlements in the territories), Rabbis for Human Rights (opposed to the occupation), Ta'ayush (a Jewish-Palestinian partnership), TANDI (Movement of

Democratic Women for Israel promoting rights for Arab women), Women in Black (opposed to the occupation), and Yesh Gvul (encouraging soldiers to refuse service in occupied territories).

This is only one event among many designed to promote collaboration and eventual peace, but not the type of event that the press appears eager to acknowledge and cover. Israelis and Palestinians marched together, hand-in-hand, and nobody got killed. If I hadn't received the e-mail, I would have had no idea that so many Israeli and Palestinian groups were working together toward a peaceful solution to the conflict. So why is the press ignoring, rather than highlighting, this type of news? Is it afraid that if it covers these rallies, it will legitimize the peace movement and, through publicizing it, increase support for it? Without the media's feedback, individuals preferring peaceful rather than military options must be feeling virtually invisible, not knowing if they are part of a large or small, active or passive segment of Israeli society. Alternatively, it could just be that the press merely views the Left as engaging in largely symbolic activities with little hope of having a real impact. The peace protests here are definitely kinder and gentler than those of my past as an American growing up in the sixties. In contrast, the press has eagerly embraced one specific aspect of the peace movement— namely, the controversy resulting from a recent ad appearing in newspapers sponsored by fifty-three Israeli reserve military officers and soldiers who say they are unwilling to fight in the occupied territories. According to the ad, the soldiers will no longer participate in missions in the territories, which they believe are designed to "control, expel, starve, and degrade an entire people." This ad subsequently inspired others, one in which opposing reservists said they "completely disassociate" themselves from an action that they view as "dangerous and anti-democratic." Certainly, this type of issue is more attractive to the press because it involves conflict and the important policy question of where patriotism ends and treason begins. Further, it resonates with historical themes dating back to the 1967 War, one of the most glorified moments in Israel's brief history. Following that conflict, some returning soldiers reported that they were shocked upon learning for the first time that Palestinians longed to return to land that they believed was rightly theirs and which, from their vantage point, had been taken by Israel. The young men had never learned this perspective in their history books; they went to war as young idealists, but returned as disillusioned adults. A few years later, during the war in Lebanon, another group of soldiers questioned the legitimacy of the conflict in which they were engaged, culminating in the formation of Yesh Gvul, the original movement that encouraged reserve soldiers to refuse to serve in the occupied territories. This movement was somewhat successful and was credited in part for Israel's subsequent decision to withdraw its forces from Lebanese territory, a result that this current generation of protesting soldiers and peace activists hope to emulate.

But it doesn't appear very likely at the moment. Clearly, the political Left has crumbled in the past year with every new report of a suicide bombing and subsequent death of Israeli citizens. After all, it's hard to promote dialogue for peace with an enemy who is slaying friends left and right—a sentiment that resonates with Israelis and Palestinians alike. The radical (and outlawed) right-wing Kach Party has even gone so far as to print stickers containing a thinly veiled threat to those who strive for peace: "No leftists, No terrorists." Nonetheless, several activist groups continue to promote dialogue and compromise, trying to establish common ground, as well as sponsoring events that, in another era and different setting, might be viewed as worthy of media coverage and public attention, and as a much-needed source of hope to a people tired of bloodshed.

WEEK 20: ENDINGS

"I survived Armageddon."

No, I'm not talking about my five months in Israel during the current intifada, but rather the slogan on a T-shirt printed by a Jaffa dealer in ancient coins who operates an ongoing archaeological site near Har Megiddo. Better known to Americans by the more familiar Greek translation, Armageddon is where the Book of Revelations says the final and ultimate battle between good and evil will ensue. Megiddo, located at the end of a long ridge of mountains, is the site of numerous settlements built on top of one another over the span of several thousand years, all guarding the Jezreel Valley and several important trade routes. Because of its strategic importance, it was also the location of numerous battles for control of the lucrative mountain pass. From the west, the winding, rising, S-shaped road appears easily defended; but from the east, the vast plains are much more vulnerable to marauding armies. Is this truly where it all will end? It's as good a guess as any, given Megiddo's history and the volatile politics of the region.

Relatively close by is one of my favorite spots in all the country—and the site of yet another unpleasant ending: the Crusader fortress of Belvoir. As the French name suggests, the fortress is indeed home to a spectacular view—perched high on a hilltop overlooking the Jordan River, the agricultural patchwork of the Jordan Valley, the Golan Heights, and the Sea of Galilee, and offering a beautiful glimpse of snow-covered Mount Hermon in the distance. Given its location, I can only imagine the dismay the Muslim troops must have felt when they stood at the bottom of the hill in the heat of summer and looked up at the formidable objective that they were expected to capture. Surrounded on three sides by a dry moat, the fourth side was considered impregnable because it faced a steep eastern slope. But during a siege that lasted some two years, the great Muslim warrior Saladin chose this side for his attack and breached the outer wall. The invaders then faced another daunting barrier, as the fortress was constructed with a second, inner wall of stone; but they penetrated that as well. No doubt, the inhabitants must have been positively shocked and terrified when they heard the shouts of invaders smashing through the last gates of their seemingly impenetrable fortress.

A far more pleasant ending was shaping up in the relative safety of Tel Aviv University, where the culmination of the semester was fast approaching. My course has been a very positive experience, and I have learned a lot about the country and its people from class discussions. The single most unexpected finding is the high degree of fatalism and low degree of political efficacy on the part of my students, made even more surprising by the fact that Tel Aviv University students in general tend to be older and more worldly than most American students. They disagree with many of the policies of the government, resent many of the restrictions imposed by the religious, deeply lament what is happening with the Palestinians, and loathe the rampant corruption. Nevertheless, when I ask what they plan to do, they uniformly shrug their shoulders and say that nothing can be done. Although Israelis generally describe themselves as assertive, if not aggressive, the students I encounter appear to completely lack confidence in their ability to influence policy in the political sphere. They may be extremely knowledgeable about current affairs, but they simply don't believe they have any control or power over what happens in their country.

A week ago, I asked students a series of questions about their perceptions of the violence and their expectations for the future. "What lies ahead in your own lives?" I asked. The dual threats of drowning in taxes and suffering from violence constituted the most common response. "How do you cope with the violence?" They told me that they go to cafés and basically just try to ignore it. But always in the back of their minds is the thought that they may have to transform suddenly from citizens to soldiers in the blink of an eye. "How many of you," I asked, "plan to leave Israel because of the violence?" Although every student has traveled or plans to travel out of the country, none admitted to harboring thoughts of leaving for good. Was social desirability or small-group conformity a factor in their responses? Perhaps, although Israelis have incredible allegiance to their country, as well as a keen ability to accept the bad with the good. Next I asked, "How many of you would not bring children into this world of violence?" This question, as I expected, elicited a strong and immediate negative reaction; I might as well have asked them if they planned to stop breathing. Family is a cornerstone of the Jewish heritage, and nothing could ever stand in the way of that. In my final question, I asked if they expected their children's lives to be better than their own.

Interestingly, none did, though several thought that their grandchildren's or great-grandchildren's lives might improve. Basically, they've given up hope for anyone born before a firm peace agreement is in place, though they believe that children born after the hoped-for peace have a chance of avoiding the shackles of resentment and hatred.

For the last class session of the semester, I made a deal with the students: I'd supply the pizza if they'd bring beverages of their choice. As has usually been the case here, a couple of minor, last-minute glitches surfaced—not the least of which was Domino's (yes, it's here, too) inability to deliver on campus. So a colleague and staff member patiently waited with 200 shekels in hand down by nearby Gate No. 5, picked up the pizzas and breadsticks, and then raced them to my fourth-floor classroom. The arrival of the food prompted a buzz of excitement, as well as the click and pop of beer bottles and soda cans opening around the room.

It was their day for questions, and they wanted to know all about my perceptions of Israel. Was I scared to come to Israel back in September? Did I consider it a third-world country? Did it seem more like America or a European country? What did Americans *really* think of Israel and Israelis? Did we feel sympathy for them? Would I ever come back? While their questions were both thought-provoking and revealing about the country's preoccupation with its image, I wasn't prepared for what was to come next. One of the students pulled a brightly wrapped package from her bag and told me that the members of the class had chipped in to purchase me a gift. When I opened the package, I was stunned; inside was an elegant pen on which they had engraved the words: "To Professor Charles Salmon, With Appreciation." Accompanying the pen was a beautiful ceramic Hamsa, a symbol of good luck (and a token, they assured me, that would protect me from any vampires roaming around Michigan). The gifts took me completely by surprise and will remain among my most treasured belongings.

Eventually, our pleasant conversation about images of Israel ended, and as the students arose from their desks and chairs, one of them, an officer in the reserves, came up to the front of the room, shook my hand, thanked me for coming to the country, and wished me luck. Suddenly, one by one, all the students came up to the front and either shook my hand or waved goodbye. I told them to be safe, and wished them good fortune in their futures. It was very personal and very emotional. At that moment, the intensity and fragility of life here was evident; I was feeling a powerful bond with strangers who, over the course of fourteen weeks of coexisting in an environment of terrorism, bombings, and shootings, had become my friends. Our paths had crossed serendipitously, and now we were about to head our separate ways in a volatile and unpredictable world.

WEEK 21: EXODUS

FROM MY EARLIEST DAYS in Tel Aviv, I had admired the Azrieli Towers, Israel's gleaming and brightly lit versions of the ill-fated Twin Towers of New York City. With one being round and the other rectangular, they were obviously fraternal, rather than identical twins, but they were nonetheless my destination tonight as I enjoyed one final night out on the town. It was my first time heading to the top of a skyscraper in the wake of 9/11, and a couple of people in the express elevator made nervous jokes about the chances of encountering a jumbo jet hurtling into the tower upon our ascent. But nothing out of the ordinary occurred, and we merely enjoyed our dinners and admired the views of the sparkling city below from our perch on the forty-ninth floor.

Upon returning to my apartment, I stayed up late to cram the last few souvenirs and items of clothing into the fourth of my huge suitcases, and managed to fill another six boxes—mostly with souvenirs. Israeli merchants would miss me dearly. Then I took one final walk around the neighborhood and beach, savoring memories of the many people and events that had made my visit so memorable.

The next day, following a final reception in my department and farewells to my landlady and newfound friends (working in my favorite juice bar, cashew stand, and ice cream booth), I prepared my departure. Quite familiar with the formidable reputation of Israeli airport security personnel, I arrived at the airport three hours before my flight, expecting the worst. In the weeks immediately following September 11, Israeli security personnel obviously were sympathetic about what had happened in the States. But at the same time, I detected a smug belief that the airport security breaches that had happened in the States could never happen here. Israel prides itself on having state-of-the-art airport security, a model for other countries to envy and emulate. However, it clearly has its own limitations. During my interrogation, a really huge, heavily armored, and winged cockroach started chasing my interrogator around the airport floor. Clearly flustered by its persistence and unpredictable trajectory, she ended the interview rather abruptly, slapped stickers on my carry-on luggage, and hurried off, leaving me free to roam in and out of the secured area—which I did more than once, just to see what might happen. Nothing did, and so once again, I left underwhelmed with the security of the aircraft that I was about to board.

My flight was uneventful, but loud and a bit strange. A group of Israeli men sitting in adjacent seats were telling stories and laughing loudly enough to be heard several rows away. Immediately in front of me, an infant screeched and screamed for more than two hours, without a break. Instead of eliciting scornful looks and muttered curses, though, the infant's cacophonous sounds instead attracted the sympathy and attention of at least a half dozen middle-aged women, who took turns holding and trying to calm the baby, and exchanging tips about various home remedies. Meanwhile, a boy from an Orthodox family crawled up and down the aisle, dragging a long trail of toilet paper in his teeth and engaging in tugs of war with various travelers along the way.

Soon, I landed in Paris for a two-day vacation, and my extended visit to Israel had finally reached its conclusion. The city was cold, dark, and rainy, and I stood shivering in the rain while trying to cram my four ridiculously large suitcases through the narrow doors of the crowded shuttle bus. Within minutes, it became clear that I wasn't in Israel any longer. Lobbies and restaurants were quiet; people stood in line patiently, without pushing, and with visible space between them. And they smiled. The atmosphere seemed to be lighter, the people heavier, and the graffiti more colorful and artistic.

Two incidents in particular illustrated the differences in my new surroundings. First, while standing in line to register at my hotel, I noticed two men simultaneously moving toward the counter to check in with the same clerk. When they realized the situation, one gentleman stopped and waved the other forward, saying, "Pardon me." Not to be outdone, the other man halted as well, and similarly waved the first man forward. This ritual went on for two more rounds. Months before, I might have been impressed with their manners and good-natured civility; but now, after five months in the Middle East, the ritual seemed almost comical. I stood there attempting to calculate the odds of something like this ever happening in Tel Aviv, but stopped when I approached negative numbers. The next day, while touring the rafters of Notre Dame Cathedral, I faced a narrow wooden staircase on which a tourist was already heading down. I started heading up, and immediately the other person stopped, backed up, and let me have the staircase all to myself. No doubt, he judged me to be rude and ill-bred, and had he known from whence I had recently arrived, he would, no doubt, have labeled me as a typically pushy Israeli—or worse. But was I? I had become accustomed to "violations" of personal space, and was not bothered by the fact that we might brush up against each other on the staircase. And I simply didn't want to wait for him to traverse the entire set of stairs. Did this make me rude and pushy? Or was he instead merely timid, or less tolerant of people in close propinquity? Yet another variant of the "terrorist" versus "patriot" semantic disagreement at work, but one that made me rethink some of the bases of my own stereotypes and attributions of behaviors.

In spite of the inclement weather, Paris was stunning. The massive architecture had a sense of solidity and permanence that I had not encountered in Tel Aviv, a city of less than one hundred years in age. Late in the afternoon, I returned to Notre Dame to sit in serenity during the angelic Vespers—when it occurred to me that I was sitting in exactly the same spot where aspiring Crusaders might have sat in the twelfth and thirteenth centuries. What could have motivated nobles and peasants in this splendid city to forsake their homes and families to engage in their "jihad" one thousand years before? I had recently seen first-hand the fate that awaited them, and I shuddered to think of the suffering they endured—and inflicted—in their ill-conceived quest. In spite of the massive social, technological, and economic changes that have rocked the world over the past nine hundred years, in some ways little has changed, at least in terms of the passions that will inspire men, women, and children to make great sacrifices for their beliefs.

Speaking of passions: having restored my sense of perspective in the ethereal spaces of the cathedral, I hopped into a cab and reached the Moulin Rouge just in time for the evening show.

Expecting a spectacle similar to what I had seen in the recent movie by the same name, I was terribly disappointed to find instead a rather pedestrian dinner-theater show, similar to what might appear at an American Midwestern casino, but with a much steeper price of admission. So much for life imitating art.

In my first weekly report, I wrote about how ridiculously lax French airport security had been at DeGaulle Airport, with children attempting to crawl through the x-ray machine, and passengers streaming through the metal detector unsearched. Since that time, the infamous Shoe Bomber had allegedly managed to pass through the cracks in the French security system—with fuses sticking out of his shoe, no less. Heads must have rolled, for this time my experience was totally different. Every bit of luggage was opened and thoroughly searched. My passport was checked at least five times, and I wasn't allowed to carry aboard a small bag that failed a weight test. As I stood and unsuccessfully attempted to negotiate with the airline personnel, three French police officers raced by, dragging a handcuffed man in tow. Inconvenienced but comforted by the intense security, I resumed my passage to the United States. This portion of the flight was far quieter and calmer than the first, and soon the familiar landmarks at O'Hare Airport in Chicago appeared in the distance.

When the tires of my plane hit American soil, waves of contradictory emotions overtook me. I missed the life and friends that I had left behind in Israel; but at the same time, I also felt an overpowering sense of pride, accomplishment, and relief. I'd made it! Swept up in the emotion of my safe return and the exhilaration of my many life-changing adventures, the only thing that perplexed me was why I had ever been reluctant to go in the first place.

TRANSITIONS

THE DAYS THAT FOLLOWED proved unexpectedly challenging: though physically in the Midwest, psychologically I was still in the Middle East. I found myself still thinking like someone in Tel Aviv, preoccupied with the conflict in Israel, but surrounded by the snow, cold, and remoteness of a grey world that had remained unchanged for five months. I maintained my connection to Israel via news on the Internet, only to find myself interpreting reports differently than I had before. In the past, a death was a death was a death; but now it mattered where and how the death occurred. Did the latest suicide—make that "homicide"—bombing of an Israeli occur in downtown Tel Aviv, or in a new settlement in one of the territories? Did the most recent shooting of a Palestinian youth occur while he was sitting in his home, or out in the streets, engaged in violence? It was as though I were in a hospital ward, viewing two people dying of lung cancer, and thinking differently about the one who contracted it from actively smoking two packs a day versus the non-smoker who became afflicted passively through second-hand smoke.

Many other changes had occurred within me as well. Living in the Holy Land had thoroughly shaken my faith in religious institutions. Whereas I had viewed religion as a wellspring of hope and support prior to my visit, I now saw it as a major cause of, rather than a solution to, many of the world's problems. Like most Americans, I was already critical of the Taliban, the Muslim fundamentalists who had kidnapped a nation of Afghanis, and of Muslim religious extremists who used the concept of a "holy war" to justify terrorist attacks on civilians in New York City. But now I had spent five months listening to a host of secular Tel Aviv acquaintances criticizing their ultra-religious countrymen. In café after café, the complaints were amazingly consistent, signifying fairly widespread dissatisfaction: "They are bleeding dry those of us who pay taxes to support them." "They are military hawks who aren't willing to fight, while pushing us to the brink of war with their settlements." "They want to make (former Prime Minister) Rabin's killer a national hero for preventing a peace that they don't want." As for Christians, I had just spent five months touring Crusader ruins and rereading tales of slaughter and treachery in the name of God and religion. Then, to cap it off, soon after my return to the States, revelations started bursting forth daily about sexual abuse and child molestation on the part of Catholic clergy—first in the United States, but soon throughout the rest of the world as well. Over the next several weeks, a cavalcade of Muslim, Jewish, and Christian leaders appeared on all the world's stages, promoting themselves and their religions as instruments of peace and love; but now, their words sounded hollow.

My well-intentioned friends, who were decidedly happy to see me home in one piece, listened politely as I shared stories and insights; but nobody really seemed to fully appreciate what I felt, or what was really going on over there. Soon, the novelty of my return tapered off completely. There was still so much to say, but little opportunity to say it; at times, I felt like I was going to burst. My sleep became restless, my eating habits were completely disrupted, and I quickly gained back much of the weight that I had lost by walking on the beach and indulging in Mediterranean fruit juices, rather than American junk food. Ironically, I found myself communicating less with local friends than I had while I was overseas and sending weekly e-mail letters. Stacks of mail from my five months abroad remained unopened on my desk for longer than I care to admit, and I struggled to keep a smile on my face while trying to readjust to life outside of Israel. At a certain point, I decided that I would simply have to return, if only to try to gain some additional sense of closure and perspective on my experience. After checking my schedule and starting to dig out from the paper rubble on top of my desk, I prepared for my return to Israel in late May. But first, I would have to survive a previously scheduled business trip to Malaysia.

I was a little apprehensive about going to a predominantly Muslim country following an extended stay in Israel—and less than nine months after September 11—but I found Malaysia to be an especially beautiful, friendly, and peaceful sliver of the world. The country is an exotic integration of Chinese, Indian, and Muslim cultures, with forward-thinking leaders who value education and technology, positioning the country as a potential leader in the Muslim world. Especially pleasant and serene was the luscious tropical island of Pulau Pinang, where I spent ten days working and talking to local residents. One day, when touring Universiti Sains Malaysia, I found myself in an unexpected conversation with a Chinese colleague about the luscious bird sanctuary on campus, which also happens to be home to dozens of venomous—and uninvited—king cobras. Apparently, it is a basic law of nature that wherever birds nest, snakes are sure to follow.

"How can this be?" I asked in astonishment. "In America, we would never sit idly by and tolerate a known enclave of dangerous snakes on a college campus" (with the notable exception of certain faculty colleagues, I thought to myself, but that's not the issue here). In the first place, university administrators would be virtually obligated to eradicate the campus of cobras, in proactive attempts to "manage risk." If not, they would most certainly face negative publicity—and even lawsuits—for failing to act on the knowledge of a potential threat to their faculty, staff, students, and visitors. And in the second place, I could almost guarantee that some sensation-seeking students would probably get tanked up some Saturday night and then head to the sanctuary to see how many of the creatures they could catch, light on fire, or otherwise maim.

"That is so cruel. Why kill snakes that have bothered no one?" my colleague asked. I started explaining the virtues of being proactive, of not waiting around to become victims, and the need for preemptive strikes, sounding more and more like a script writer for Ariel Sharon and George W. Bush with every word.

"You can't kill every snake," my Malaysian colleague said admonishingly, "and besides, they don't deserve to die merely because they are poisonous and Americans are scared of them." In a flash, a conversation about local snakes had become a metaphor for global wars against terrorism, and a Chinese professor in this predominantly Muslim country was lecturing me about the futility and cruelty of trying to exterminate that which we regard as a threat. Why not attempt to gain understanding and tolerance, and learn to coexist with that which we find so foreign and threatening? Why cling to the belief that killing will beget an end to killing? A valid point, especially given a long-term perspective, but not what a person wants to hear when writhing in agony from a snakebite. We often do indeed believe that we can kill every snake, and even exhibit this mindset proudly to the world in every action film that we produce. Rambo, Dirty Harry, and the Terminator have not become cultural icons by "charming," but rather by pulverizing their snake-like enemies. But in real life, it's rarely the case that we really can kill every snake, and even if we manage to kill the most vituperative ones, it does seem that we only stir up more anger in the ones that survive. Armed with new perspective, I headed back to Israel for a second look.*

---

*Ironically, right before I left Malaysia, a young, disoriented cobra slithered into the building in which I was staying, where two workers summarily beat it to death with sticks. The incident was a classic illustration of what often happens when idealism is subjected to the test of reality.

THE RETURN

DURING MY EARLIER VISIT, I had an impression that the ongoing conflict in Israel was to some degree a personal vendetta between Ariel Sharon and Yasser Arafat, who, like Holmes and Moriarty, were locked in a titanic struggle and intent upon hurling themselves together into the abyss. This time around, it seems as though many more of their compatriots have joined them, though not necessarily by choice. In Tel Aviv, Palestinian suicide bombers have eliminated any shred of detachment and insularity that may have existed during my earlier stay. Israelis are depressed, frustrated, fatalistic, scared, and most of all, angry—at Yasser Arafat in particular and Palestinians in general. Hatred is palpable, as is resignation that no end to the conflict is in sight. Most residents are only one or two persons removed from a victim of violence. With every suicide bombing or shooting, the circle of those affected ripples outward, giving people little time to grieve before preparing for the next bad news. And it has come almost daily over the past few months.

The recent wave of violence has damaged the city in many ways: first, by exacerbating trends already headed in negative directions. The tourism industry has been flattened, hotel occupancy is way down, sidewalks are less crowded, and some businesses are cutting back on their hours or closing altogether. Amichay, the owner-manager of the hotel at which I am staying this time, reports that more than 230 stores have closed on Dizengoff Street over the last two years. He himself recently launched what he calls a "Yasser Arafat/Osama bin Laden" sale, in a last-ditch attempt to attract foreign tourists to his hotel. So far, it isn't working especially well; occupancy is only about one-third this month, and is expected to be lower in July. Many more elderly men and women, as well as musicians, now dot the sidewalks, hands extended in hopes of attracting a spare shekel or two from a charitable passerby. The sight is particularly commonplace near ATM machines, where the obvious visual contrast between the haves (bejeweled and bedecked in expensive designer clothes) and have-nots (sprawled on the sidewalks in mere rags) is often quite stunning, though probably no different from what can be seen in many major cities these days.

Security here is unquestionably tighter. Pairs of border police with automatic weapons slung on their backs are frequently seen on the streets, examining suspicious double-parked cars and occasionally interrogating wayward drivers. And, in a sign of the times, the popular annual book fair—normally held outdoors at Rabin Square—was, for the first time, moved indoors this year for reasons of security. Whereas four months ago shopping malls, supermarkets, theaters, banks, and government buildings were guarded, now many individual retail stores and most cafés and restaurants boast their own guards as well. Friends tell me that in order to collect unemployment here, one has to be willing to work if a job becomes available. Since nearly every place is hiring security guards these days, security is a boom industry for the unemployed. Guards come in nearly all shapes and sizes, as well as degrees of thoroughness and seriousness. Some are Israeli, some are Russian, and several are women; but all appear desperate to make their jobs more meaningful as they pace, stand, lean, sit, yawn, talk, people-watch, and rummage through purses all day long. A few of them, particularly those resembling members of the Mossad, look as though they could break people in half. Most of these are young, stern, and muscular—equipped with sunglasses, pistols, and nasty, hand-held metal-detecting wands. In contrast, some other guards look as though they might actually wake up later in the day. Many of these can be seen sitting and daydreaming in the smaller cafés before struggling to stand, offering a cursory glance inside a purse or a wave of a hand, and then returning to their comfortable roost. Still others are mere youths who joke with fellow teens and occasionally fail to notice someone wandering behind them and through an entrance.

Hiring all of these new guards is not cheap, and most eating establishments pass along this cost to the consumer through a "security fee" added to the bill, which often already includes a 12 percent "service fee." I've paid as little as one shekel and as much as four for security in different cafés, leading me to wonder what additional measure of security I am actually getting for the higher amount. Does the more expensive security guard have a larger caliber gun? A higher-degree belt in karate or tae kwon do? More highly honed skills in rummaging through a suspicious-looking cosmetics case? Doubtful— though what's perhaps more interesting is that some people believe that cafés and restaurants are actually profiting by charging a security fee. Like acorns, little amounts of shekels here and there can grow into something considerably larger over the course of several months—certainly much larger than the salaries that many of these people are receiving. Three issues seem to be on everyone's mind: the violence, the settlements, and the fact that the whole world seems to be watching what is going on here.

SUICIDE BOMBS

Amazing as it may sound, suicide bombings seem to have become somewhat routinized here over the past several months. Perhaps the best indicator of this is that local bookies actually have begun taking bets on where the next bombing will occur, with Jerusalem the odds-on favorite during my first week back. A macabre development to be sure, but also indicative of the degree to which these events, like horse races and basketball games, are now happening with a certain predictability. Although people are shocked and scared by news reports of the bombings, they return to their routines more quickly than in the days of the initial attacks. Radio stations still change their format and play quiet, calming music following a bombing, but for a shorter period of time before resuming their normal programming. Health and public safety officials have become better prepared and more experienced, systematic, and efficient in dealing with the aftermath of bombings.

Earlier this week, I drove to Jerusalem with a friend, and arrived in the city just in time for the bustle of morning rush-hour traffic. We heard on the news that five suspected terrorists from the West Bank had made it into Israel the day before, intent on being suicide bombers in Jerusalem, Haifa, and some other locations. Helicopters had circled Jerusalem overnight looking for signs of the suspects, but to no avail.

While having breakfast in the elegant American Colony

Hotel in East Jerusalem, home to most foreign correspondents in the city, I overheard a terse but brief cell phone conversation at a nearby table of European reporters: "Hello . . . How many are dead? . . . Turn off Al-Jazeera, turn on a Hebrew station, and call me back." Learning that a bombing had just claimed (at the time) at least seventeen lives, I tracked down a cab and asked the driver to take me as close as he could to the scene. The driver, a Palestinian, dropped me off a few blocks away, unwilling to get any closer for fear, he said, of getting beaten up. I walked the rest of the distance to the site and talked to several people about what had happened. It seems that a Palestinian from a West Bank refugee camp had boarded a bus (at about the same time that I had arrived in the city) and blown himself up, killing schoolchildren and elderly men and women, Arabs as well as Jews, in the process. The explosion had been powerful enough to lift the bus off the ground and rip it apart, sending pieces of flesh and metal flying high into the air. Prime Minister Ariel Sharon made a rare appearance at the scene and condemned the act of terrorism, which occurred just before American President Bush was scheduled to offer his proposal for an end to the conflict. Now, as I watched highly specialized work crews managing the aftermath of the explosion, workers lifted larger pieces of debris onto trucks to be carted away. Others swept the smaller pieces of debris—metal, glass, paper, human flesh—into neat piles, where their co-workers, wearing gloves, got down on their knees to sort through them, looking for pieces of bodies. A while later, the workers began sifting through leaves and branches of nearby trees, looking for slivers of body parts there as well. Both groups of workers were attempting to retrieve all parts of all bodies—a canon of Jewish religious laws regarding proper burial, but an impossibility with this particular form of murder. As these men completed their work, large machines lumbered in, some sweeping the street and others providing one final cleansing. Police on horseback rerouted traffic around the carnage, while groups of Arab boys leaned against temporary fences and called over to the many reporters and photographers at the scene. The whole scene appeared amazingly and disturbingly routine, almost like construction workers assembling a new section of highway. But of course, these workers were working on a far more gruesome project, and having to repeat the same grisly routine week after week.

By one count, this was the seventieth suicide bombing since the start of the Second Intifada, the ninth involving a bus. The seventy-first would happen the very next morning, also in Jerusalem. This time, near the evening rush hour, the bomber stepped out of a red car and ran toward a crowded bus stop, holding a backpack filled with a bomb. Before suspicious police could nab him, he detonated it, killing at least seven and injuring more than forty others.

In this environment, feelings of unpredictability and lack of control amplify the actual effect of the bomb blast. Sure, Israelis know that more people die in auto accidents or from heart attacks than from terrorism, but they expect those kinds of deaths and have some illusion of control over them. But they don't believe that anything can be done to truly control or prevent the bombings, and when terrorism becomes a near-daily occurrence, people in Tel Aviv and Jerusalem live in a near-perpetual state of anxiety. They can never quite be sure whether the car that just pulled up in front of their building is laden with bombs, whether the bus on which they are sitting is about to pick up a suicide bomber at the next stop, or whether the café they're in will be stormed by someone wearing a belt full of explosives.

I was very surprised to read the other day that fifty-eight of Israel's national parks (including the famous Masada, Ein Gedi, Caesarea, and Beit She'an) may have to close for awhile, an action that may cause "permanent damage" to the sites. Why? According to the *Jerusalem Post*, a newspaper intended primarily for non-Israelis, there is not enough money to keep them open, because tourism dollars are down, and the security situation has depleted tourism funding.

This was disappointing news, but it jogged something in my memory from my previous visit. Upon checking through a thick stack of papers, I found an article about how, a few months ago, the new minister of tourism decided to divert his agency's funding away from tourism promotion and into the construction of new settlements in the West Bank. I shared this information with some friends in Tel Aviv, who simply shook their heads, cursed, and talked about how this was just one more example of how settlements are "ruining our lives."

The issue of settlements has increasingly become a flash point: the line of demarcation between the Israeli political Right and the political Left.

To the Right, the settlements represent the new Zionism, a rekindling of the spirited movement that made Israel what it is today. To these people, the borders of the "country of Israel"— created by the United Nations in 1948—are pretty much irrelevant in comparison to the borders of the "land of Israel" —promised by their God more than five thousand years ago. Some of the settlers believe that what they are doing will accelerate the coming of their Messiah and fulfill a Biblical prophesy. Others believe they are merely exercising a divine right to settle anywhere in their Biblical land, from which their ancestors were driven thousands of years ago. Another group sees the settlements as a first line of defense against hostile Arab enemies who still harbor dreams of pushing the Israelis into the sea. A related group believes settlements represent a continuation of the secular Zionist movement that secured the land in the first place, leading to the creation of the country of Israel. Finally, still others, mostly secular Israelis and/or Russian immigrants, are young families unmotivated by religious or philosophical beliefs and instead simply looking for inexpensive housing.

Those on the political Left, on the other hand, oppose the settlements and urge their Israeli brethren to return to the pre-1967 border of Israel. A few point out that the settlements are being established in violation of international law, and hence reflect illegal spending and building. Others, the hard-core seculars, consider it ridiculous that ancient religious texts could be used as a justification for what they see as unadulterated "land grabbing" in contemporary times. One self-acclaimed liberal described this apocryphal account of a Palestinian who lost his land to a religious settlement:

> Palestinian: "How can you take my land? I have deeds, legal documents!"
> Settler: "So; I have documents from God."

But most opponents are simply pragmatic, believing that the settlements are wrong, that they cause anger, and that they stoke the fires for much of the violence that ensues. Public opinion polls show that a majority of Israelis—not just a few leftists—would give up the settlements in exchange for peace, suggesting that support for the settlements is coming from a politically powerful minority rather than a democratic majority. To people adhering to this perspective, the settlers may or may not be patriotic "new Zionists" or "defenders of Israel," but they are pushing the country closer and closer to full-scale war.

In a fascinating investigative report on Channel One the other day, a TV journalist described how he had spent a year following the activities of a group of religious settlers who wanted to take control of a nearby hill and construct a new settlement on it. How could they annex the land when they didn't own it, and the minister of defense was publicly promising that his government was not allowing the construction of any new settlements? They made a few unsuccessful attempts before eventually figuring out the solution: they complained about poor cell phone connections. Bad phone service meant their phone company needed to build an antenna on a high spot of land nearby, such as on the hill that the village coveted. Once there was an antenna, it had to have a fence around it to protect it. Once there was a fence with something to protect, a guard had to be hired. Because the guard happened to be religious, he needed at least nine more men with whom to pray in order to conform with Jewish custom. In order for the ten men to be able to pray there regularly, they had to have someplace to sleep, so temporary housing was set up. Once there was housing, water and electricity needed to be added. What started as a solitary antenna to boost cell phone signals had now become a veritable community, which was then given a Biblical name.

In some viewers, the story may have elicited pride and stirrings of old nationalism; similar approaches were used to secure land prior to 1948 in the original Zionist movement, and hence these contemporary settlers are viewed as both patriotic and clever. Yet in others, the news broadcast may have elicited outrage, as it is obvious that settlers and government officials are collaborating with a wink and a nod, telling the world one thing and doing the opposite under the cloak of a different pretext. Is this example an aberration? It doesn't appear so. The reporter estimated that some fifty similar settlements had been built in the last eighteen months. Another journalist told me that people in Tel Aviv "have no idea" how many settlements are being built in the West Bank. Apparently, the government has been on a frenzied building spree in the last several months. "Why?" I asked. According to the journalist, the settlements will be used as bargaining chips in a land-for-land swap. In this swap, Palestinians will be expected to relinquish any claims they may have on Israeli lands, or any right to return to those lands, and in exchange, they will be given land taken from them by the settlers. Or, if the government is feeling more confident, it will say that it can't possibly force its citizens to give up all of their communities, houses, and belongings, so new national boundaries will have to be established that take into account how Israel has expanded since 1948.

It's hard to tell if this is an accurate or merely cynical explanation and prediction. Nevertheless, it is indisputable that the government is spending an enormous sum of money to build new houses, highways, and infrastructure in the territories— not exactly the kind of activity that suggests that the government is about to freely hand over the land to create a new Palestinian state. If it does hand it over, then this all may someday be viewed as just a gigantic waste of money, especially if the settlements are destroyed when the settlers leave them. Meanwhile, one could make a strong case that American taxpayers have a lot at stake here. The United States gives Israel between $2 and $3 billion a year, and certainly much of this money has either been used to build settlements or to allow domestic dollars to be freed up for this purpose. But this may only be the start. My friends tell me that if the settlers are forced to relinquish their homes and move back into the "country" of Israel, they will be given reparations to compensate for their move, much of which will likely come from the United States, one way or another.

THE PUBLIC MOOD

Although everyone here seems angry about the ongoing violence, some blame the Palestinians exclusively while others apportion some of the blame to their own government for its apparent failure to make progress toward a political solution. But sharing disparaging thoughts privately with fellow Israelis and listening to outsiders publicly express disparaging comments about the country are two entirely different matters. Sensitivity to external criticism appears to be at an all-time high, and many Israelis are positively dismayed by international commentary, which they view as shockingly unsupportive of their situation. They see themselves as canaries in the coal mine: the first to suffer the effects of emerging global terrorism. As such, they expect to feel appreciated for serving as sentinels on the frontlines of a new war; instead they find themselves accused of being agents of colonization, oppression, and even apartheid.

Earlier in the year, the United Nations General Assembly voted 133–4, with 16 abstentions, to approve a resolution labeling Israel as an "occupying power" and demanding that it cease "willful killing, torture, and extensive destruction of property." In spite of the lopsided vote, this criticism was summarily dismissed and seemingly ignored because the U.N. is routinely viewed here as dominated by Arabs and anti-Semites. And international condemnation of Israel's recent military actions in Jenin and Bethlehem were deflected as well with parallels to American incursions in Afghanistan and resulting "collateral damage" to civilian populations in that country.

In recent days, however, criticisms from America's Ted Turner and Britain's Cherie Blair and Jack Straw really struck a raw nerve. Their assertions that Israelis were contributing to and perhaps even partly responsible for the conflict, as opposed to being blameless victims of it, were denounced as blatantly anti-Semitic and led to demands for apologies and threats of boycotts. At about the same time that all of this was happening, Israel's Minister of Communication labeled CNN's coverage of the violence as "evil, biased, and unbalanced," and threatened to remove the channel from cable systems in the country. More than any other countries in the world, America and Britain matter to Israel, and what American and British media moguls and political leaders believe and say is considered vitally important to the very existence of this country.

But not all external criticism is viewed as mere anti-Semitism. Israelis attribute some of it to the situation being so hopelessly complex that only an insider can understand it. The phrase "it's complicated," has become a clichéd response to virtually all of my questions, with people unable to provide answers without first pointing out that knowledge of some tragic, yet obscure event from the second or fourth century is essential for a proper understanding of current affairs. The bottom line of this rationalization is that outsiders can't possibly possess the requisite sophistication, understanding or empathy for their criticisms to be taken seriously.

Others attribute external criticism to the success of Palestinian public relations efforts to influence global opinion. For example, when I ask how Israelis are suffering in the conflict, I am likely to hear a detailed and lengthy reply. But if I ask about Palestinian suffering that I may have read or heard about, the common reply is a warning that I should be careful not to fall into the trap of Palestinian propaganda. Palestinians are masters of propaganda, I am told, and Europeans in particular have fallen for it hook, line, and sinker. "Should I be equally concerned about falling into a trap of Israeli government propaganda as well?" I ask. "Why should you be? We are telling the truth," people explain with a shrug.

But Life Goes On

Nevertheless, in spite of the bombings, the depressed mood, the arguments over the settlements and the disappointment in international opinion, life goes on much as it did during my first visit. Young people still visit and restaurants, and attend movies, but they also party into the wee hours of dawn at private homes, settings less vulnerable to attack. Adults still frequent cafes, though now they give more thought to where to sit in hope of maximizing safety in the event of a terrorist act. The beaches are actually far more packed than when I was here before in winter, as thousands of Tel Aviv families flock to the Sea to cool off during this very hot June. A recent food festival reportedly drew more than 100,000 persons—far more than most peace rallies, interestingly enough—while a wonderful International Youth Film Festival attracted foreign filmmakers and scores of young moviegoers. In an ironic sort of way, the conflict is arousing previously dormant feelings of nationalism, much as in the post–9/11 United States, as people are uniting in the face of a common enemy. New public policy proposals are springing up, policies intended to rekindle the Zionist movement, reform processes of immigration and citizenship, and further strengthen the State against enemies within as well as without. With pride, people tell me that the hard times could have brought about the worst, but they are instead bringing about the best in young and old alike. In general, many people support their country and continue to maintain public lives if only to make it absolutely clear to terrorists that they will not be intimidated, they will not be pushed into the sea. Time and time again, I hear the words, "What choice do we have? We must keep living our lives; we won't be intimidated . . ."

EPILOGUE

As I ATTEMPTED TO WRITE a concluding chapter for this work, grounded in key historical and political considerations of the region, I found myself getting more and more lost in contradiction with every new fact and interpretation that I uncovered. After I returned to the States the first time, I spent months reading newspaper articles, scholarly essays, and policy critiques. I read about the many original visions of Israel, from hard-core secular to hard-line religious, and started to understand why, no matter what conclusion I might draw, someone could legitimately tell me I was wrong. There was no "real" story of a single people, but a multitude of contradictory accounts of numerous groups with conflicting agendas. And I'm just talking about Israelis here, not even including in the mix the multitudinous perspectives of the Palestinians and neighboring Arabs. This point was driven home when, soon after arriving for my second visit, I watched the award-winning film *Kedma*, the story of European Jews pressed into military service immediately upon arriving in the land now known as

Israel. One patron cried, while another got up and left in disgust. Afterwards, I learned that the movie triggered memories of what young, idealistic Israelis had learned as children about the Zionist movement and the Arabs. For some, their childhood reflections were now being exposed as myths of Zionist propaganda, while for others early memories were being revitalized through renewed sentiments of nationalism. The more conflicting information and anecdotes I accumulated in my effort to contextualize this book, the more I felt like I was standing squarely in the middle of an unfamiliar crossroads, looking in two directions: at a past with no agreement on fact, and at a future with no apparent resolution in sight.

At the same time, I noticed that the tone and focus of my writing changed between my first and second visits. In my first visit, I hadn't set out to write about politics and conflict because I knew that Americans were already getting a steady diet of this information at home. I had expected to be jumping out of the post–9/11 frying pan and into a Middle Eastern fire, but instead had only positive experiences, and rarely—if ever—felt at risk.

Certainly, some of my own views and attitudes changed in the intervening months between visits. And I was finding that a little knowledge can indeed be a dangerous thing. In my second visit, I was now more likely to challenge a conclusion that I had heretofore accepted due to my admitted unfamiliarity with the culture and history of the land. I found myself being swept up in the abstract politics of conflict and less satisfied with any explanation that was filtered through a monochromatic lens. I had wonderful new friends, cherished memories, and newly acquired insight about suffering and hope, but I also had strong feelings about heretofore unfamiliar social policies with which I now disagreed. I questioned whether I had failed to look at my environment with a sufficiently critical eye during my first visit, or whether I was now being excessively critical during my second. And I wondered how different my stories would have been if I had taught at the religious Bar-Ilan University instead of the secular Tel Aviv University, or regularly met for lunch and dinner with Palestinian, rather than Israeli, friends and colleagues.

I suppose the quandary that I was in was a decent metaphor for the situation in the entire region, which only makes me wonder how any citizen of one country can even begin to hope to understand the complexities of the situation in another, here or anywhere else. First-hand experience raises new questions and threatens old stereotypes, but it is still incomplete and selective. The alternative is to rely on news, which is a recycled sampling of someone else's equally incomplete and selective first-hand experiences. I found American news reports to be extraordinarily divergent from my own observations in Israel and very misleading in their depiction of daily life in this country. What gets reported about Israel—or indeed any country, including the United States—is in no way, shape, or form "All" the news that's fit to print. Instead, it's obsession with conflict and celebrity— the dramatic tip of the much larger, more representative, and yet largely unreported, iceberg.

In the end, my own experiences suggest to me that the real story of Israel is not about bombs and bullets or Ariel Sharon or Yasser Arafat but rather about people such as Hannah, who made me tea and tirelessly told me stories of her grandson, Dror; Muhammad, the Palestinian taxi driver who believes he could sit down with his Jewish neighbors in Jerusalem and solve the conflict in a day; Grace and Ike, the Nigerians whose wedding I attended in Jaffa; and of course my delightful students at Tel Aviv University, who so patiently taught me so much. I feel so incredibly privileged to have had the opportunity, as an outsider in both a religious and cultural sense, to experience first-hand the delicacies of cherished ordinary life that I could never have tasted through my usual media diet back in the States. I sincerely hope that the burgeoning conflict currently threatening to engulf the globe does not deter others from sharing similar experiences to mine.

As for my own story, I make no claims that my depiction of life in Tel Aviv is any more "authentic" than a *New York Times*, CNN, or *Lansing State Journal* report. I lived in one city, characterized by its particular culture and norms; lived in a particular neighborhood, characterized by a certain socioeconomic status; met with a regular group of friends, characterized by a particular orientation to religious, family, and intellectual life; participated in an infinitesimally small subset of all possible permutations of social experience in the midst of a few million people (most of whom I never met); read only a few of the many local publications, each characterized by a particular political viewpoint; and made interpretations of what I saw on the basis of my own preconceptions and resulting misperceptions as a Christian American outsider in an unfamiliar land. But while this particular report may not have any greater claim to authenticity or reality than a conventional news story, it may, on the other hand, offer a glimpse of life in Israel that might otherwise go unseen, and amplify a voice or two that might otherwise go unheard. There are multiple legitimate perspectives on any reality; this one was mine.